Don't Shoot the Dog!

"Pryor explains why punishment—the 'take *that*!' style of trying to get people to change—so often fails, and she describes the specific methods that *do* work. This book will do more for human relations than all the well-meaning but vague pep talks to love thy neighbor, or improve thyself, for Pryor shows how to move from *intention* to *results*."
—Carol Tavris, Ph.D, author of *Anger*

"Karen Pryor has been a pioneer . . . anyone who wants to be more effective in rearing children, teaching, or managing his or her own behavior will find her book very useful."
—B. F. Skinner

"A wealth of relevant anecdotes . . . Pryor's treatment of ten situations by each of eight methods is a perfect illustration of behavior modification."
—*Publishers Weekly*

READERS RAVE:

"A pivotal work in the fields of human psychology and dog training . . . A must-read for anyone interested in human or canine behavior modification."
—Deborah Jones, Ph.D, assistant professor,
Kent State University, and owner,
Planet Canine Dog Training School

DON'T SHOOT THE DOG!

THE NEW ART OF
TEACHING AND TRAINING

REVISED EDITION

KAREN PRYOR

RINGPRESS

Originally published in English by
Bantam Books, NY
Copyright © 1999 Karen Pryor.

This edition published by
Ringpress Books Ltd,
A division of Interpet
Vincent Lane, Dorking,
Surrey, RH4 3YX

Cover design: Sara Howell

Reprinted 2019

ISBN 978 1 86054 238 1

Printed and bound in Great Britain
by CPI Group (UK) Ltd, Croydon, CR0 4YY

To my mother, *Sally Ondeck*
my stepmother, *Ricky Wylie*
and
Winifred Sturley,
my teacher and friend

Contents

In which we learn of the ferocity of Wall Street lawyers; of how to—and how not to—buy presents and give compliments; of a grumpy gorilla, a grudging panda, and a truculent teenager (the author); of gambling, pencil chewing, falling in love with heels, and other bad habits; of how to reform a scolding teacher or a crabby boss without their knowing what you've done; and more.

How to conduct an opera; how to putt; how to handle a bad report card. Parlor games for trainers. Notes on killer whales, Nim Chimpsky, Zen, Gregory Bateson, the Brearley School, why cats get stuck in trees, and how to train a chicken.

Orders, commands, requests, signals, cues, and words to the wise; what works and what doesn't. What discipline isn't. Who gets obeyed and why. How to stop yelling at your kids. Dancing, drill teams, music, martial arts, and other recreational uses of stimulus control.

Eight methods of getting rid of behavior you don't want, from
messy roommates to barking dogs to bad tennis to harmful addictions, starting with Method 1: Shoot the Animal, which definitely
works, and ending with Method 8: Change the Motivation, which
is more humane and definitely works too.

What it all means. Reading minds, coaching Olympic teams, how
happiness can affect corporate profits, ways to deal with other
governments, and other practical applications of reinforcement
theory.

From the dolphin tanks to everyone's backyard: dog owners
around the world put away the choke chain and pick up the
clicker. Long-term benefits: accelerated learning, precision, reliability, better communication, and fun. The Great Internet Canine
Hot Dog Challenge; some truly fetching horses; a pilot pilot program; and clicking and autism. Changing the world one click at
a time.

Foreword

This book is about how to train anyone—human or animal, young or old, oneself or others—to do anything that can and should be done. How to get the cat off the kitchen table or your grandmother to stop nagging you. How to affect behavior in your pets, your kids, your boss, your friends. How to improve your tennis stroke, your golf game, your math skills, your memory. All by using the principles of training with reinforcement.

These principles are laws, like the laws of physics. They underlie all learning-teaching situations as surely as the law of gravity underlies the falling of an apple. Whenever we attempt to change behavior, in ourselves or in others, we are using these laws, whether we know it or not.

Usually we are using them inappropriately. We threaten, we argue, we coerce, we deprive. We pounce on others when things go wrong and pass up the chance to praise them when things go right. We are harsh and impatient with our children, with each other, with ourselves even; and we feel guilty over that harshness. We know that with better methods we could accomplish our ends faster, and without causing distress, but we can't conceive of those methods. We are just not attuned to the ways in which modern trainers take advantage of the laws of positive reinforcement.

Whatever the training task, whether keeping a four-year-old quiet in public, housebreaking a puppy, coaching a team, or memorizing a poem, it will go faster, and better, and be more fun, if you know how to use positive reinforcement.

The laws of reinforcement are simple; you can put the whole business on a blackboard in ten minutes and learn it in an hour. Applying these laws is more of a challenge; training by reinforcement is like a game, one dependent upon quick thinking.

Anyone can be a trainer; some people are good at it from the very start. You do not need special qualities of patience, or a forceful personality, or a way with animals or children, or what circus trainer Frank Buck used to call the power of the human eye. You just need to know what you're doing.

There have always been people with an intuitive understanding of how to apply the laws of training. We call them gifted teachers, brilliant commanding officers, winning coaches, genius animal trainers. I've observed some theater directors and many symphony orchestra conductors who are wonderfully skilled at using reinforcement. These gifted trainers don't need a book to be able to take advantage of the laws that affect training. For the rest of us, however, those of us muddling along with an uncontrolled pet or at cross-purposes with a child or coworker, a knowledge of how reinforcement really works can be a godsend.

Reinforcement training is not a system of reward and punishment—by and large modern trainers don't even use those words. The concept of reward and punishment carries a great freight of emotional associations and interpretations, such as desire and dread and guilt and shoulds and ought to's. For example, we give rewards to others for things we did ourselves—such as ice cream to a child to make up for a scolding. We also tend to think we know what a reward should be: ice cream, for example, or praise. But some people don't like ice cream, and praise from the wrong person or for the wrong reason may hurt. In some cases praise from a teacher may guarantee ridicule from classmates.

We expect people to do the right thing without reward. Our teenage daughter should wash the dishes because that's her duty to us. We are angry if children or employees break things, steal, arrive late, speak rudely, and so on, because they should know better. We punish, often long after the behavior occurred—sending people to prison being a prime example—thus creating an event that may have no effect on future behavior, and which in fact is merely retribution. Nevertheless we think of such punishment as education, and people easily refer to it in that way: "I taught him a lesson."

Modern reinforcement training is based not on these folk beliefs but on behavioral science. Scientifically speaking, reinforcement is an event that (a) occurs during or upon completion of a behavior; and (b) increases the likelihood of that behavior occurring in the future. The key elements here are two: the two events are connected in real time—the behavior engenders the reinforcement—and then the behavior occurs more frequently.

Reinforcers may be positive, something the learner might like and want more of, such as a smile or a pat, or they might be negative, something to avoid, such as a yank on a leash or a frown. What's critical is that there is a temporal relationship between them—the behavior occurs, then the reinforcer occurs, and subsequently the behavior that brought the good result or averted the bad occurs more often. In fact, the definition works in both directions, like a feedback loop: If the behavior does *not* increase, then either the reinforcer was presented too early or too late, or the payoff you selected was *not* reinforcing to that individual.

In addition, I believe there's an important difference between reinforcement *theory*, the science, and reinforcement *training*, a specific application of that science. Research shows that following a behavior with a pleasant consequence increases the behavior. That's true; but in practice, to get the sensational results we trainers have now come to expect, the reinforcer has to occur in the very instant the behavior is taking place. Bingo! Now! In the instant, in real time, you, the learner, need to know that what you're doing *right now* has won you a prize.

Modern trainers have developed some great shortcuts for reinforcing instantaneously: primarily the use of a marker signal to identify the behavior. This revised version of *Don't Shoot the Dog!* is about the laws of reinforcement, some practical ways to use those laws in the real world, and the grassroots movement called, at least at present, clicker training, which is taking the technology into new and unexplored terrain.

I first learned about training with positive reinforcement in Hawaii, where in 1963 I signed on as head dolphin trainer at an oceanarium, Sea Life Park. I had trained dogs and horses by traditional methods, but dolphins were a different proposition; you cannot use a leash or a bridle or even your fist on an animal that just swims away. Positive reinforcers—primarily a bucket of fish— were the only tools we had.

A psychologist outlined for me the principles of training by reinforcement. The art of applying those principles I learned from working with the dolphins. Schooled as a biologist, and with a lifelong interest in animal behavior, I found myself fascinated, not so much with the dolphins as with what could be communicated between us—from me to the animal *and* from the animal to me— during this kind of training. I applied what I'd learned from dolphin training to the training of other animals. And I began to notice some applications of the system creeping into my daily life. For example, I stopped yelling at my kids, because I was noticing that yelling didn't work. Watching for behavior I liked, and reinforcing it when it occurred, worked a lot better and kept the peace too.

There is a solid body of scientific theory underlying the lessons I learned from dolphin training. We shall go considerably beyond theory in this book, since as far as I know, the rules for *applying* these theories are largely undescribed by science and in my opinion often misapplied by scientists. But the fundamental laws are well established and must be taken into account when training.

The study of this body of theory is variously known as behavior modification, reinforcement theory, operant conditioning, behaviorism, behavioral psychology, and behavior analysis: the branch of psychology largely credited to Harvard professor Skinner.

I know of no other modern body of scientific information that has been so vilified, misunderstood, misinterpreted, overinterpreted, and misused. The very name of Skinner arouses ire in those who champion "free will" as a characteristic that separates man from beast. To people schooled in the humanistic tradition, the manipulation of human behavior by some sort of conscious technique seems incorrigibly wicked, in spite of the obvious fact that we all go around trying to manipulate one another's behavior all the time, by whatever means come to hand.

While humanists have been attacking behaviorism and Skinner himself with a fervor that used to be reserved for religious heresies, behaviorism has swelled into a huge branch of psychology, with university departments, clinical practitioners, professional journals, international congresses, graduate studies programs, doctrines, schisms, and masses and masses of literature.

And there have been benefits. Some disorders—autism, for example—seem to respond to shaping and reinforcement as to no other treatment. Many individual therapists have been extremely successful in solving the emotional problems of patients by using behavioral techniques. The effectiveness, at least in some circumstances, of simply altering behavior rather than delving into its origins has contributed to the rise of family therapy, in which every family member's behavior is looked at, not just the behavior of the one who seems most obviously in distress. This makes eminent good sense.

Teaching machines and programmed textbooks derived from Skinnerian theory were early attempts to shape learning step by step and to reinforce the student for correct responses. These early mechanisms were clumsy but led directly to CAI, Computer-Assisted Instruction, which is great fun because of the amusing nature of the reinforcers (fireworks, dancing robots) and highly effective because of the computer's perfect timing. Reinforcement programs using tokens or chits that can be accumulated and traded for candy, cigarettes, or privileges have been established in mental

r institutions. Self-training programs for weight
r habit changes abound. Effective educational sys-
principles of shaping and reinforcement, such as
ching and Direct Instruction, are making inroads in
And biofeedback is an interesting application of rein-
forcem to training of physiological responses.

Academicians have studied the most minute aspects of conditioning. One finding shows, for example, that if you make a chart
to keep track of your progress in some self-training program, you
will be more likely to maintain new habits if you solidly fill in a
little square every day on the chart, rather than just putting a
check mark in the square.

This absorption with detail has valid psychological purposes,
but one does not often find much good *training* in it. Training is a
loop, a two-way communication in which an event at one end of
the loop changes events at the other, exactly like a cybernetic
feedback system; yet many psychologists treat their work as
something they do *to* a subject, not *with* the subject. To a real
trainer, the idiosyncratic and unexpected responses any subject
can give are the most interesting and potentially the most fruitful
events in the training process; yet almost all experimental work is
designed to ignore or minimize individualistic responses. Devis-
ing methods for what Skinner named *shaping*, the progressive
changing of behavior, and carrying out those methods, is a creative process. Yet the psychological literature abounds with shaping programs that are so unimaginative, not to say ham-handed,
that they constitute in my opinion cruel and unusual punishment. Take, for example, in one recent journal, a treatment for
bed-wetting that involved not only putting "wetness" sensors in
the child's bed but having the therapist spend the night with the
child! The authors had the grace to say apologetically that it was
rather expensive for the family. How about the expense to the
child's psyche? This kind of "behavioral" solution is like trying to
kill flies with a shovel.

Schopenhauer once said that every original idea is first ridiculed, then vigorously attacked, and finally taken for granted.

As far as I can see, reinforcement theory has been no exception. Skinner was widely ridiculed years ago for demonstrating shaping by developing a pair of Ping-Pong-playing pigeons. The warm, comfortable, self-cleansing, entertainment-providing crib he built for his infant daughters was derided as an inhumane "baby box," immoral and heretical. Rumors still go around that his daughters went mad, when in fact both of them are successful professional women and quite delightful people. Finally, nowadays many educated people treat reinforcement theory as if it were something not terribly important that they have known and understood all along. In fact most people *don't* understand it, or they would not behave so badly to the people around them.

In the years since my dolphin-training experiences, I have lectured and written about the laws of reinforcement in academic and professional circles as well as for the general public. I've taught this kind of training to high school, college, and graduate students, to housewives and zookeepers, to family and friends, and, in weekend seminars, to several thousand dog owners and trainers. I have watched and studied all kinds of other trainers, from cowboys to coaches, and I've noticed that the principles of reinforcement training are gradually seeping into our general awareness. Hollywood animal trainers call the use of positive reinforcement "affection training" and are using these techniques to accomplish behaviors impossible to obtain by force such as many of the behaviors of pigs and other animals in the movie *Babe*. Many Olympic coaches nowadays use positive reinforcement and shaping, instead of relying on old-fashioned browbeating, and have achieved notable improvements in performance.

Nowhere, however, have I found the rules of reinforcement theory written down so that they could be of use in immediate practical situations. So here they are, explained in this book as I understand them and as I see them used and misused in real life.

Reinforcement training does not solve all problems—it will not fatten your bank account, it cannot save a bad marriage, and it will not overhaul serious personality disorders. Some situations, such as a crying baby, are not training problems and require other kinds of solutions. Some behaviors, in animals and people, have genetic components that may be difficult or impossible to modify by training. Some problems are not worth the training time. But with many of life's challenges, tasks, and annoyances, correct use of reinforcement can help.

Using positive reinforcers in one situation may show you how to use them in others. As a dolphin researcher whom I worked with sourly put it, "Nobody should be allowed to have a baby until they have first been required to train a chicken," meaning that the experience of getting results with a chicken, an organism that cannot be trained by force, should make it clear that you don't need to use punishers to get results with a baby. And the experience should give you some ideas about reinforcing baby behavior you want.

I have noticed that most dolphin trainers, who must develop the skills of using positive reinforcers in their daily work, have strikingly pleasant and agreeable children. This book will not guarantee you agreeable children. In fact, it promises no specific results or skills. What it will give you is the fundamental principles underlying all training, and some guidelines on how to apply these principles creatively in varying situations. It may enable you to clear up annoyances that have been bothering you for years, or to make advances in areas where you have been stymied. It will certainly, if you wish, enable you to train a chicken.

There seems to be a natural order to reinforcement training. These chapters come in the sequence in which training events, from simple to complex, really take place, and this is also the sequence in which people seem to learn most easily to be real trainers. The organization of this book is progressive in order to develop a comprehensive understanding of training with positive reinforcers. Its applications, however, are meant to be practical. Throughout the book's chapters real-life situations are offered as illustrations. Specific methods should be treated as suggestions or inspirations, rather than as definitive instructions.

DON'T SHOOT
THE DOG!

1

Reinforcement: Better than Rewards

What Is a Positive Reinforcer?

A reinforcer is anything that, occurring in conjunction with an act, tends to increase the probability that the act will occur again.

Memorize that statement. It is the secret of good training.

There are two kinds of reinforcers: positive and negative. A positive reinforcer is something the subject wants, such as food, petting, or praise. A negative reinforcer is something the subject wants to avoid—a blow, a frown, an unpleasant sound. (The warning buzzer in a car if you don't fasten your seat belt is a negative reinforcer.)

Behavior that is already occurring, no matter how sporadically, can always be intensified with positive reinforcement. If you call a puppy, and it comes, and you pet it, the pup's coming when called will become more and more reliable even without any other training. Suppose you want someone to telephone you—your offspring, your parent, your lover. If he or she doesn't call, there isn't much you can do about it. A major point in training with reinforcement is that you can't reinforce behavior that is not occurring. If, on the other hand, you are always delighted when your loved ones do call, so that the behavior is positively reinforced, the likelihood is that the incidence of their calling will probably increase. (Of course, if you apply negative reinforcement—"Why haven't you called, why do I have to call you, you never call me," and so on, remarks likely to annoy—you are setting up a situation in which the caller avoids such annoyance by not calling you; in fact, you are training them not to call.)

Simply offering positive reinforcement for a behavior is the most rudimentary part of reinforcement training. In the scientific literature, you can find psychologists saying, "Behavioral methods were used," or, "The problem was solved by a behavioral approach." All this means, usually, is that they switched to positive reinforcement from whatever other method they were using. It doesn't imply that they used the whole bag of tricks described in this book; they may not even be aware of them.

Yet switching to positive reinforcement is often all that is necessary. It is by far the most effective way to help the bed-wetter, for example: private praise and a hug for dry sheets in the morning, when they do occur.

Positive reinforcement can even work on yourself. At a Shakespeare study group I once belonged to I met a Wall Street lawyer in his late forties who was an avid squash player. The man had overheard me chatting about training, and on his way out the door afterward he remarked that he thought he would try positive reinforcement on his squash game. Instead of cursing his errors, as was his habit, he would try praising his good shots.

Two weeks later I ran into him again. "How's the squash game?" I asked. A look of wonder and joy crossed his face, an expression not frequently seen on Wall Street lawyers.

"At first I felt like a damned fool," he told me, "saying 'Way to go, Pete, attaboy,' for every good shot. Hell, when I was practicing alone, I even patted myself on the back. And then my game started to get better. I'm four rungs higher on the club ladder than I've ever been. I'm whipping people I could hardly take a point from before. And I'm having more fun. Since I'm not yelling at myself all the time, I don't finish a game feeling angry and disappointed. If I made a bad shot, never mind, good ones will come along. And I find I really enjoy it when the other guy makes a mistake, gets mad, throws his racquet—I know it won't help *his* game, and I just smile. . . ."

What a fiendish opponent. And just from switching to positive reinforcement.

Reinforcers are relative, not absolute. Rain is a positive reinforcer to ducks, a negative reinforcer to cats, and a matter of indifference, at least in mild weather, to cows. Food is not a positive reinforcer if you're full. Smiles and praise may be useless as reinforcers if the subject is trying to get you mad. In order to be reinforcing, the item chosen must be something the subject wants.

It is useful to have a variety of reinforcers for any training situation. At the Sea World oceanariums, killer whales are given many reinforcers, including fish (their food), stroking and scratching on different parts of the body, social attention, toys, and so on. Whole shows are run in which the animals never know which behavior will be reinforced next or what the reinforcer will be; the "surprises" are so interesting for the animals that the shows can be run almost entirely without the standard fish reinforcers; the animals get their food at the end of the day. The necessity of switching constantly from one reinforcer to another is challenging and interesting for the trainers, too.

Positive reinforcement is good for human relationships. It is the basis of the art of giving presents: guessing at something that will be definitely reinforcing (guessing *right* is reinforcing for the giver, too). In our culture, present giving is often left to women. I even know of one family in which the mother buys all the Christmas presents to and from everyone. It causes amusement on Christmas morning, brothers and sisters saying, "Let's see, this is from Anne to Billy," when everyone knows Anne had nothing to do with it. But it does not sharpen the children's skills at selecting ways to reinforce other people.

In our culture a man who has become observant about positive reinforcement has a great advantage over other men. As a mother, I made sure that my sons learned how to give presents. Once, for example, when they were quite young, seven and five, I took them to a rather fancy store and had them select two dresses, one each, for their even younger sister. They enjoyed lolling about in the plush chairs, approving or disapproving of each dress as she modeled it. Their little sister enjoyed it too; and she had the ultimate veto power. And so, thanks to this and similar exercises, they all learned how to take a real interest in what *other* people want; how to enjoy finding effective positive reinforcers for the people you love.

Negative Reinforcement

A reinforcer is something that *increases* a behavior; but it doesn't have to be something the learner wants. Avoiding something you dislike can be reinforcing, too. Laboratory research shows that behavior can be increased by aversive stimuli if a change in behavior will make the aversive stimulus go away. Such stimuli are called negative reinforcers: things a person or animal will work to avoid.

Negative reinforcers may consist of the mildest of aversive stimuli—a derisive glance from a friend when you make a poor joke, or a slight draft from an air conditioner that causes you to get up and move to another chair. However, even very extreme aversives, from public humiliation to electric shock, may function as negative reinforcers as well as being punishing experiences. We may experience being yelled at as highly punitive, but we also quickly learn to come in to work the back way when the boss who has often yelled at us is standing in the front door.

Negative reinforcers are aversives that can be halted or avoided by changing behavior. As soon as the new behavior starts, the aversive stimulus stops, and thus the new behavior is strengthened. Suppose that while sitting in my aunt's living room, I happen to put my feet on the coffee table as I would at home. My aunt raises a disapproving eyebrow. I put my feet on the floor again. Her face relaxes. I feel relieved.

The raised eyebrow was an aversive stimulus acting as a negative reinforcer. Because I was able to halt the aversive stimulus, the new behavior—keeping my feet on the floor—is more likely to occur again, at least at my aunt's house, but possibly in other houses, too.

Training can be done almost entirely with negative reinforcers, and much traditional animal training is done exactly that way. The horse learns to turn left when the left rein is pulled, because the annoying pressure in its mouth ceases when the turn is made. The lion backs onto a pedestal and stays there, to avoid the intrusive whip or chair held near its face.

Negative reinforcement, however, is *not* the same as punishment. So what is the difference? In the first edition of this book I wrote that punishment is an aversive stimulus that occurs after the behavior it was meant to modify, and therefore it can have no effect on the behavior. "A boy being spanked for a bad report card may or may not get better report cards in the future, but he surely can't change the one he has just brought home." Indeed, when we punish with intent, we frequently do it far too late, but that is not the actual difference between punishment and negative reinforcement.

Modern behavior analysts identify punishment as any event that *stops* behavior. A baby starts to put a hairpin into the electric socket. His mother grabs him and/or slaps his hand away from the socket: this life-threatening behavior has to be interrupted *now.* The behavior stops. Lots of other things may start—the baby cries, the mother feels bad, and so on—but the hairpin-in-electric-outlet behavior ceases, at least for that moment. That's what punishment does.

B. F. Skinner was more precise. He defined punishment as what happens when a behavior results in the loss of something desirable—the pleasure of investigating if this object can fit into that hole, a popular pastime with babies—*or* when the behavior results in the delivery of something undesirable. However, in both cases, while the ongoing behavior stops, there is no predictable outcome in the future. We know that reinforcers strengthen behavior in the future, but a punisher will not result in *predictable* changes.

For example, will grabbing the baby or smacking his hand, even if his mother's timing is perfect, guarantee that the baby won't try sticking things into outlets again? I doubt it. Ask any parent. What really happens is that we pick up small objects, we put covers over the wall outlets, or we move furniture in front of them, and eventually the baby outgrows this particular urge.

The behavior analysts look at it this way. Reinforcement and punishment are each a *process,* defined by results. Negative reinforcers can be used effectively to train behavior, and even though aversive stimuli are involved, the process can be relatively benign Here (with thanks to llama expert Jim Logan) is a nice use of the negative reinforcer with a semidomestic animal, the llama, kept in the United States as pets and elsewhere as pack animals and for their wool.

Llamas are timid and shy, like horses. Unless handled a lot when young, they can be hard to approach So, while operant conditioning with a food reinforcer works splendidly with llamas, if a llama is too skittish to come close enough to a person to take the food, here's what modern llama trainers do. They use a clicker as a signal to tell the llama that what it is doing has earned a reinforcer, but the primary or real reinforcer is the removal of a negative reinforcer, an aversive.

In effect, you say to the llama, "Will you stand still if I approach within thirty feet? Yes? Good. I'll click my clicker and turn and go farther away.

"Now will you stand still if I approach within twenty-five feet? Yes? Good. I'll click and go away."

Using the click to mark the behavior of standing still, with the scary person turning and going away again as the reinforcer, one can sometimes get within touching distance in five or ten minutes. The llama, as it were, is in control. As long as it stands still, it can make you go away! So it stands still, even when the person is right next to it.

When one has touched the llama several times and then retreated, the ice is broken. This person is no longer as scary. Now it's time for the feed bucket. The communication loop becomes "May I touch you while you stand still? Yes? Click and here's some delicious food." And the llama is on its way to earning positive reinforcers, including food and scratching and petting, with its splendid new behavior of standing still instead of heading for the next county.

This use of retreat, or easing back when the desired behavior occurs, is an important aspect of most of the so-called "horse whisperer" techniques. In most of these methods the trainer works with a loose horse in a confined area and proceeds in a relatively short time to transform a horse in flight to a horse calmly accepting a human. The horse, once perhaps completely wild, becomes so calm, even accepting a saddle and rider, that the total effect is magical.

Trainers who use these techniques often have superstitious explanations for what is happening; and while many have formed the habit of making some sound or motion that functions as the marker signal or the conditioned reinforcer, few are consciously aware of doing so. Nevertheless, it is not magic at work; it is the laws of operant conditioning.

While negative reinforcement is a useful process, it's important to remember that each instance of negative reinforcement also contains a punisher. When you pull on the left rein, until the moment that the horse turns, you are punishing going straight ahead. Overuse of negative reinforcers and other aversives can lead to what Murray Sidman, Ph.D., calls "fallout," the undesirable side effects of punishment (see Chapter 4).

Timing of Reinforcers

As already stated, a reinforcer must occur in conjunction with the act it is meant to modify. The timing of the arrival of the reinforcer is information. It tells the learner *exactly* what it is you like. When one is trying to learn, the informational content of a reinforcer becomes even more important than the reinforcer itself. In coaching athletes or training dancers, it is the instructor's shouted "Yes!" or "Good!," marking a movement as it occurs, that truly gives the needed information—not the debriefing later in the dressing room.

Laggardly reinforcement is the beginning trainer's biggest problem. The dog sits, but by the time the owner says "Good dog," the dog is standing again. What behavior did "Good dog" reinforce? Standing up. Whenever you find yourself having difficulties in a training situation, the first question to ask yourself is whether you are reinforcing too late. If you are working with a person or an animal and are caught up in the thick of the action, it sometimes helps to have someone else watch for late reinforcers.

We are always reinforcing one another too late. "Gee, honey, you looked great last night" is quite different from the same comment said at the moment. The delayed reinforcer may even have deleterious effect ("What's the matter, don't I look great now?"). We have a touching trust in the powers of words to cover our lapses in timing.

Reinforcing too early is also ineffective. At the Bronx Zoo the keepers were having trouble with a gorilla. They needed to get it into its outdoor pen in order to clean the indoor cage, but it had taken to sitting in the doorway, where with its enormous strength it could prevent the sliding door from being closed. When the keepers put food outside, or waved bananas enticingly, the gorilla either ignored them or snatched the food and ran back to its door before it could be shut. A trainer on the zoo staff was asked to look at the problem. He pointed out that banana waving and the tossing in of food were attempts to reinforce behavior that hadn't occurred yet. The name for this is *bribery*. The solution was to ignore the gorilla when it sat in the door, but to reinforce it with food whenever it did happen to go out by itself. Problem solved.

Sometimes, I think, we reinforce children too soon under the misimpression that we are encouraging them ("Atta girl, that's the way, you almost got it right"). What we may be doing is reinforcing trying. There is a difference between trying to do something and doing it. Wails of "I can't" may sometimes be a fact, but they may also be symptoms of being reinforced too often merely for trying. In general, giving gifts, promises, compliments, or whatever for behavior that hasn't occurred yet does not reinforce that behavior in the slightest. What it does reinforce is whatever was occurring at the time: soliciting reinforcement, most likely.

Timing is equally important when training with negative reinforcers. The horse learns to turn left when the left rein is pulled, but only if the pulling stops when it does turn. The cessation is the reinforcer. You get on a horse, kick it in the sides, and it moves forward; you should then stop kicking (unless you want it to move faster). Beginning riders often thump away constantly, as if the kicking were some kind of gasoline necessary to keep the horse moving. The kicking does not stop, so it contains no information for the horse. Thus are developed the iron-sided horses in riding academies that move at a snail's pace no matter how often they are kicked.

The same applies to people getting nagged and scolded by parents, bosses, or teachers. If the negative reinforcer doesn't cease the instant the desired result is achieved, it is neither reinforcing nor information. It becomes, both literally and in terms of information theory, "noise."

Watching football and baseball on TV, I am often struck by the beautifully timed reinforcers that the players receive again and again. As a touchdown is made, as the runner crosses home plate, the roar of the crowd signals unalloyed approval; and the instant a score is made or a game is won, just watch the frenzied exchange of mutual reinforcers among the players. It is quite different for actors, especially movie actors. Even on stage the applause comes after the job is done. For movie actors, except for occasional response from a director or camera operator or grip, there is no timely reinforcement; fan letters and good reviews, arriving weeks or months later, are pallid compared with all of Yankee Stadium going berserk at the moment of success. No wonder some stars often exhibit a seemingly neurotic craving for adulation and thrills; the work can be peculiarly unsatisfying because the reinforcers, however splendid, are always "late."

Size of Reinforcer

Beginning trainers who use food reinforcement with animals are often confused as to how big each reinforcer should be. The answer is: as small as you can get away with. The smaller the reinforcer, the more quickly the animal eats it. Not only does this cut down on waiting time, it also allows for more reinforcers per session, before the animal becomes satiated. In 1979 I was hired as a consultant by the National Zoological Park in Washington, D.C., to teach positive reinforcement techniques to a group of zoo employees. One of the keepers in my training class complained that her training of the panda had been proceeding too slowly. I thought this odd because intuitively I felt that pandas—big, greedy, active animals—should be easy to train with a reinforcer of food. I watched a session and found that while the keeper was gradually succeeding in shaping a body movement, she was giving the panda a whole carrot for each reinforcement. The panda took its own sweet time eating each carrot, so that in fifteen minutes of valuable keeper time it had earned only three reinforcers (and was incidentally getting tired of carrots). A single slice of carrot per reinforcement would have been better.

In general, a reinforcer that constitutes one small mouthful for that animal is enough to keep it interested—a grain or two of corn for a chicken, a quarter-inch cube of meat for a cat, half an apple for an elephant. With an especially preferred food you can go even smaller—a teaspoon of grain for a horse, for example. Keepers at the National Zoo have trained their polar bears to do many useful things, such as moving to another cage on command, with raisins.

A trainer's rule of thumb is that if you are going to have only one training session a day, you can count on the animal working well for about a quarter of its rations; you then give it the rest for free. If you can get in three or four sessions a day, you can divide the normal amount of food into about eighty reinforcers and give twenty or thirty in each session. Eighty reinforcers seems to be about the maximum for any subject's interest during any one day. (Perhaps that's why slide trays usually hold eighty slides; I know I always groan if a lecturer asks the projectionist for the second tray of slides.)

The difficulty of the task also has some effect on the size of the reinforcer. At Sea Life Park we found it necessary to give each of our whales a large mackerel for their Olympic-effort, twenty-two-foot straight-up jump. They simply refused to do it for the usual reinforcer of two small smelt. For people, sometimes if not always, harder jobs get bigger rewards. And how we hate it when they don't, if we are the ones doing the hard job.

Jackpots

One extremely useful technique with food or any other reinforcement, for animals or people, is the jackpot. The jackpot is a reward that is much bigger, maybe ten times bigger, than the normal reinforcer, and one that comes as a surprise to the subject. At an ad agency where I once worked we had the usual office party at Christmas, as well as informal celebrations to signalize the completion of a big job or the signing of a new client. But the president was also in the habit of throwing one or two totally unexpected parties a year. Suddenly in midafternoon he would stride through all the offices, yelling for everyone to stop working. The switchboard was closed down, and in came a procession of caterers, musicians, bartenders, champagne, smoked salmon, the works: just for us and for no special reason. It was an unexpected jackpot for fifty people. It contributed vastly, I thought, to the company's high morale.

A jackpot may be used to mark a sudden breakthrough. In the case of one horse trainer I know, when a young horse executes a difficult maneuver for the first time, the man leaps from its back, snatches off saddle and bridle, and turns the horse loose in the ring—a jackpot of complete freedom, which often seems to make the new behavior stick.

Paradoxically, a single jackpot may also be effective in improving the response of a recalcitrant, fearful, or resistant subject that is offering no desirable behavior at all. At Sea Life Park we were doing some U.S. Navy–funded research that involved reinforcing a dolphin for new responses, instead of old, previously trained behaviors. Our subject was a docile animal named Hou that rarely offered new responses. When she failed to get reinforced for what she did offer, she became inactive, and finally in one session she went twenty minutes offering no responses at all. The trainer finally tossed her two fish "for nothing." Visibly startled by this largesse, Hou became active again and soon made a movement that could be reinforced, leading to real progress in the next few sessions.

I had the same experience as that dolphin myself once. When I was fifteen, my greatest pleasure in life was riding lessons. The stables where I rode sold tickets, ten lessons on a ticket. From my allowance I could afford one ticket a month. I was living with my father, Philip Wylie, and my stepmother, Ricky, at the time; and although they were very good to me, I had entered one of those adolescent periods in which one practices being as truculent and disagreeable as possible for days on end. One evening the Wylies, being loving and ingenious parents, told me that they were pretty tired of my behavior, and that what they had decided to do was reward me.

They then presented me with a brand-new, extra, free riding ticket. One of them had taken the trouble of going to the stables to buy it. Wow! An undeserved jackpot. As I recall, I shaped up on the spot, and Ricky Wylie confirmed that memory as I was writing this book many years later.

Why the unearned jackpot should have had such abrupt and long-reaching effects, I do not fully understand: Perhaps someone will do a Ph.D. dissertation on the matter someday and explain it to us. I do know that the extra riding ticket instantly relieved in me some strong feelings of oppression and resentment, and I suspect that's exactly how that dolphin felt, too.

Conditioned Reinforcers

It often happens, especially when training with food reinforcers, that there is absolutely no way you can get the reinforcer to the subject during the instant it is performing the behavior you wish to encourage. If I am training a dolphin to jump, I cannot possibly get a fish to it while it is in midair. If each jump is followed by a thrown fish with an unavoidable delay, eventually the animal will make the connection between jumping and eating and will jump more often. However, it has no way of knowing which aspect of the jump I liked. Was it the height? The arch? Perhaps the splashing reentry? Thus it would take many repetitions to identify to the animal the exact sort of jump I had in mind. To get around this problem, we use conditioned reinforcers.

A conditioned reinforcer is some initially meaningless signal—a sound, a light, a motion—that is deliberately presented before or during the delivery of a reinforcer. Dolphin trainers have come to rely on the police whistle as a conditioned reinforcer; it is easily heard, even underwater, and it leaves one's hands free for signaling and fish throwing. With other animals I frequently use a cricket, the dime-store party toy that goes *click-click* when you press it, or a particular praise word, selected and reserved for the purpose of acting as a conditioned reinforcer: "Good dog," "Good pony." Schoolteachers often arrive at some such ritualized and carefully rationed word of commendation—"That's fine" or "Very good"—for which the children anxiously work and wait.

Conditioned reinforcers abound in our lives. We like to hear the phone ring or see a full mailbox, even if half our calls are no fun or most of our mail is junk mail, because we have had numerous occasions to learn to relate the ringing or the envelopes to good things. We like Christmas music and hate the smell of dentists' offices. We keep things around us—pictures, dishes, trophies—not because they are beautiful or useful but because they remind us of times when we were happy or of people we love. They are conditioned reinforcers.

Practical animal training that uses positive reinforcement should almost always begin with the establishment of a conditioned reinforcer. Before the start of any real training of behavior, while the subject is doing nothing in particular, you teach it to understand the significance of the conditioned reinforcer by pairing it with food, petting, or other real reinforcers. You can tell, incidentally, at least with animals, when the subject has come to recognize your signal for "Good!" It visibly startles on perceiving the conditioned reinforcer and begins seeking the real reinforcer. With the establishment of a conditioned reinforcer, you have a real way of communicating exactly what you like in the animal's behavior. So you do not need to be Dr. Dolittle to talk to the animals; you can "say" an amazing amount with such trained reinforcement

Conditioned reinforcers become immensely powerful. I have seen marine mammals work long past the point of satiety for conditioned reinforcers, and horses and dogs work for an hour or more with few primary reinforcers. People, of course, work endlessly for money, which is after all only a conditioned reinforcer, a token for the things it can buy—even, or perhaps especially, people who have already earned more money than they can actually spend, who have accordingly become addicted to the conditioned reinforcer.

One can make a conditioned reinforcer more powerful by pairing it with several primary reinforcers. The subject at that moment may not want food, say, but if the same reinforcing sound or word has also been associated deliberately with water, or some other needs or pleasures, it retains its usefulness and then some. My cats hear "Good girl!" when their supper dish is put down, when they are petted, when they are let in and out, and when they do little tricks and get treats for them. Consequently, I can use "Good girl!" to reinforce getting off the kitchen table, without having to follow up with an actual reinforcer. Probably the reason money is so reinforcing for us is that it can be paired with practically everything. It is an extremely generalized conditioned reinforcer.

Once you have established a conditioned reinforcer, you must be careful not to throw it around meaninglessly or you will dilute its force. The children who rode my Welsh ponies for me quickly learned to use "Good pony!" only when they wanted to reinforce behavior. If they just wanted to express affection, they could chat to the pony any way they liked, except in those words. One day a child who had just joined the group was seen petting a pony's face while saying "You're a good pony." Three of the others rounded on her instantly: "What are you telling him that for? He hasn't done anything!" Similarly one can and should lavish children (and spouses, parents, lovers, and friends) with love and attention, unrelated to any particular behavior; but one should reserve praise, specifically, as a conditioned reinforcer related to something real. There are plenty of such real events deserving praise, a reinforcer that is abundantly exchanged in happy families. False or meaningless praise, however, is soon resented, even by tiny children, and loses any power to reinforce.

Click!

Marine mammal trainers use conditioned reinforcers, usually the sound of a whistle, to train whales, dolphins, seals, and polar bears. The concept was first brought to marine mammal parks and to U.S. Navy dolphin trainers in the 1960s by Keller Breland, a graduate student of B. F. Skinner. Breland called the whistle a "bridging stimulus," because, in addition to informing the dolphin that it had just earned a fish, the whistle bridged the period of *time* between the leap in midtank—the behavior that was being reinforced—and swimming over to the side to collect one's pay.

The behavior analytic literature acknowledged these two aspects of the conditioned reinforcer. But there were more values to be uncovered. In the 1990s more and more animal trainers started using operant conditioning, shaping, positive reinforcement, and conditioned reinforcers, and so did the general public, with dog owners leading the way (see Chapter 6). Because the dog owners used a plastic boxed metal clicker as a conditioned reinforcer, they began calling what they were doing *clicker training* and themselves, clicker trainers.

The click, as it is used by clicker trainers, has several unresearched functions besides being a conditioned reinforcer and being a bridging stimulus between earning the food and getting the food. First and foremost it constitutes what Ogden Lindsley, Ph.D., has called an *event marker*. It identifies for the trainee exactly what behavior is being reinforced. But it does more than that. It puts control in the hands, paws, fins, whatever, of the learner. After a while the subject no longer just repeats the behavior; the subject exhibits intention. "Hey! I made you click! Watch me, I'm going to do it again!" Clicker trainers speak of that shift as the moment when "the light bulb goes on." This moment is extremely reinforcing for trainer and trainee alike.

Ellen Reese, Ph.D., pointed out to me that the conditioned reinforcer, as it is used by clicker trainers, is also a termination signal. It means "Job's done." As Gary Wilkes says, "The click ends the behavior." That's reinforcing in itself. It is, however, sometimes a shock to traditional trainers: It doesn't seem natural, somehow, that the way to train a dog to hold on to a dumbbell forever is to click it for holding the dumbbell, whereupon it is permitted to drop the dumbbell instantly and eat slices of hot dog.

The philosopher Gregory Bateson, who worked at Sea Life Park for some years, maintained that operant conditioning was just a system for communicating with an alien species. Indeed, it can be. Another major value of the marker signal is that it can be used to communicate specific information. Police officer Steve White told me of sending his German shepherd patrol dog to search for a thrown object that had landed on top of a six-foot-tall clump of bushes. The dog searched the ground fruitlessly for a long time. Then, when it happened to raise its head, Steve clicked. The dog instantly sniffed the air at head height, alerted to a whiff of the target, and began searching around the area while scenting further upward, even standing on its hind legs to do so. Thus with no further help from Steve, the dog located the object, crashed on top of the bushes, and got it.

The "Keep Going" Signal

Another aspect of Steve's communication with his dog was that Steve used the click as a reinforcer that was *not* a termination signal; instead it was a "keep going" signal. The click reinforced the upward sniffing and kept the search behavior going, since the lost object had not yet been found. In this book's first edition I wrote of being able to use the conditioned reinforcer several times with no actual reinforcer until the end. I said this because we sometimes did it with dolphins at Sea Life Park, during long-duration behaviors or behavior chains. What I failed to realize at the time was that we in fact used two (at least two) conditioned reinforcers or marker signals: one, the whistle, meaning all of the above— "That's right, food's coming, go get the food over there, job's done"—and a second, a muted whistle meaning "That's right, but the job's not over yet."

Many of the novice clicker trainers I worked with in the 1990s were what author Morgan Spector calls "crossover" trainers (that is, well skilled in correction-based training, and trying to change over to shaping and positive reinforcement). I found that they were all too willing to give clicks but no treats, to the point where the significance of the click was extinguished. It was necessary to stress "One click, one treat" as a general rule, in order to teach people to shape behavior efficiently.

However, there are many situations in real life where some interim reinforcing stimulus can be very useful, as with Steve White's patrol dog. One answer is to use a different reinforcing stimulus to tell the trainee, "That's right, and keep going." Interestingly, a "keep going" signal does not have to be linked directly with a primary reinforcer. Just start inserting it somewhere before the terminating click, and the learner will soon recognize it as a signal leading toward an eventual reinforcer.

Then you can get fancy and use it as an informative marker signal within a chain, without actually stopping the chain. For example, in dog agility competition, dogs are sent one by one over an obstacle course, against the clock. The owner has to tell the dog which obstacle to take next, all at a dead run. I've seen a dog clear one obstacle and then be visibly confused, as if he didn't hear the cue clearly. Is it the tunnel, or the jump? The head swiveled back and forth, and the owner yelled "Yes!" as the dog looked toward the jump. The dog veered instantly and took the correct obstacle.

As with a terminating click, it doesn't matter what kind of stimulus was used: a clicker, a whistle, a shout, or a wave. What counts is the fact that the stimulus was not just hopeful encouragement or cheerleading, which may distract the animal or accidentally reinforce the wrong behavior, but a well-established and precisely used conditioned reinforcer

Conditioned Aversive Signals

A timely conditioned positive reinforcer tells the recipient, "What you are doing now is good and will gain you something, so do it some more." You can also establish a conditioned aversive, or punisher, which communicates, "What you are doing now is not good, and something bad will happen unless you stop."

Conditioned aversive stimuli are more effective than threats. Some subjects—cats come to mind—are unresponsive to shouts and scolding. However, a friend of mine quite accidentally cured her cat of clawing the couch by establishing "No!" as a conditioned aversive stimulus. One day in the kitchen she happened to drop a large brass tray, which fell right next to the cat. She cried "No!" as the tray fell, just before it landed with a loud clatter. The cat, dreadfully startled, jumped into the air with all its fur on end

The next time the cat clawed the couch, the owner exclaimed "No!" and the cat, looking horrified, desisted immediately. Two more repetitions were enough to end the behavior permanently.

Reprimands are a necessary part of existence. Using positive reinforcement as your main teaching tool does not mean you cannot use "No!" when you need to, for example when the baby pokes at the wall outlet. However, some trainers use this real-life circumstance to justify their own general and abundant use of "correction" in instruction. In doing so they make two mistakes. First, they view correction as if it were equivalent in value to positive reinforcement, without taking into account the other effects it has on the learner (see "Punishment," Chapter 4); and second, they use those reprimands and punishers without establishing a warning signal, or conditioned aversive stimulus.

The trick to making "No!" effective is to establish it as a conditioned negative reinforcer. For example, anyone who feels it necessary to use a choke chain on a dog should *always* say "no" as the dog does the wrong thing, and then pause before yanking on the chain, giving the dog a chance to avoid the aversive by changing its behavior. To just yank on the chain without a warning turns the yank into a simple punishment, with no predictable effect on future behavior and a potential cumulative effect on the dog's willingness to work at all. A third popular error, continuing to yank while the dog is back in position, simply punishes both behaviors.

Failing to use a conditioned negative reinforcer increases the number of actual aversives that take place in correction-based training. It also slows up the learning. Conventional dog and horse trainers sometimes take far longer than reinforcement trainers—months and even years longer—to establish reliable behaviors, not just because they rely on punishment, which stops behavior rather than starting it, but also because they employ aversives without using a conditioned negative reinforcer, necessitating hundreds of repetitions before the animal sorts out what it is supposed to be doing.

A special case of the conditioned aversive signal has recently become popular among dog trainers: the no-reward marker, often the word "Wrong," spoken in a neutral tone. The idea is that when the dog is trying various behaviors to see what you might want, you can help him by telling him what *won't* work, by developing a signal that signifies "That will not be reinforced."

B. F. Skinner's definition of punishment—taking away something desirable—means that the "Wrong" signal is, unavoidably, a conditioned punisher, since it means that reinforcers are not available. Does it also provide information and thereby become reinforcing? In the dog training community, I am seeing special cases where the "Wrong" signal is useful. If your dog has a sizable repertoire of fully shaped behaviors and cues—if, in short, it is a highly sophisticated trainee—you can establish the "Wrong" word as a cue for variable behavior, meaning "Save your strength, that's a blind alley, try something else."

This only works if the learner has already been reinforced often for variable behavior and for actively searching for new ways to make you click. Where people run into trouble with this tricky stimulus is when they use it with an inexperienced dog that doesn't understand what is wanted. In this case people tend to use the signal as if it were a choke collar: Tell the dog to sit, it doesn't sit, bam—"Wrong." If the signal has indeed been established as meaning no reinforcer is available, then "not sitting" is punished. But that doesn't mean that sitting is now going to happen. In fact, the results are apt to be the same as with any other punisher—highly unpredictable. The dog may quit responding altogether and slink away, or give up and start looking for its own reinforcers, resulting in unsuitable behavior such as barking, pulling on the leash, sniffing the ground, scratching, and in general taking its attention elsewhere.

Schedules of Reinforcement

There is a popular misconception that if you start training a behavior by positive reinforcement, you will have to keep on using positive reinforcers for the rest of the subject's natural life; if not, the behavior will disappear. This is untrue; constant reinforcement is needed just in the *learning* stages. You might praise a toddler repeatedly for using the toilet, but once the behavior has been learned, the matter takes care of itself. We give, or we should give, the beginner a lot of reinforcers—teaching a kid to ride a bicycle may involve a constant stream of "That's right, steady now, you got it, *good!*" However, you'd look pretty silly (and the child would think you were crazy) if you went on praising once the behavior had been acquired.

In order to maintain an already-learned behavior with some degree of reliability, it is not only not necessary to reinforce it every time; it is vital that you do *not* reinforce it on a regular basis but instead switch to using reinforcement only occasionally, and on a random or unpredictable basis.

This is what psychologists call a variable schedule of reinforcement. A variable schedule is *far more* effective in maintaining behavior than a constant, predictable schedule of reinforcement. One psychologist explained it to me this way: If you have a new car, one that has always started easily, and you get in one day and turn the key and it doesn't start, you may try a few more times, but soon you are going to decide something is wrong and go call the garage. Your key-turning behavior, in the absence of the expected immediate reinforcement, quickly extinguishes, or dies out. If, on the other hand, you have an old clunker that almost never starts on the first try and often takes forever to get going, you may try and try to start it for half an hour; your key-turning behavior is on a long, variable schedule and is thereby strongly maintained.

If I were to give a dolphin a fish every time it jumped, very quickly the jump would become as minimal and perfunctory as the animal could get away with. If I then stopped giving fish, the dolphin would quickly stop jumping. However, once the animal had learned to jump for fish, if I were to reinforce now the first jump, then the third, and so on at random, the behavior would be much more strongly maintained; the unrewarded animal would actually jump more and more often, hoping to hit the lucky number, as it were, and the jumps might even increase in vigor. This in turn would allow me to selectively reinforce the more vigorous jumps, thus using my variable schedule to shape improved performance. But even some professional animal trainers fail to make good use of variable schedules of positive reinforcement; it seems to be a peculiarly difficult concept for many people to accept intellectually. We recognize that we don't need to go on punishing misbehavior if the misbehavior stops, but we don't see that it's not necessary or even desirable to reward correct behavior continuously. We are less sure of ourselves when aiming for disciplined response through positive reinforcement.

The power of the variable schedule is at the root of all gambling. If every time you put a nickel into a slot machine a dime were to come out, you would soon lose interest. Yes, you would be making money, but what a boring way to do it. People like to play slot machines precisely because there's no predicting whether nothing will come out, or a little money, or a lot of money, or *which* time the reinforcer will come (it might be the very first time). Why some people get addicted to gambling and others can take it or leave it is another matter, but for those who do get hooked, it's the variable schedule of reinforcement that does the hooking.

The longer the variable schedule, the more powerfully it maintains behavior. Long schedules work against you, however, if you are trying to eliminate a behavior. Unreinforced, any behavior will tend to die down by itself; but if it is reinforced from time to time, however sporadically—one cigarette, one drink, one giving in to the nagger or whiner, the behavior, instead of being extinguished, may actually be strongly maintained by a long, variable schedule. That is how the ex-smoker who sneaks an occasional cigarette can go back to being a heavy smoker in a day.

We have all seen people who inexplicably stick with spouses or lovers who mistreat them. Customarily we think of this as happening to a woman—she falls for someone who is harsh, inconsiderate, selfish, even cruel, and yet she loves him—but it happens to men, too. Everyone knows such people, who, if divorced or otherwise bereft of the nasty one, go right out and find someone else just like him or her.

Are these people, for deep psychological reasons, perpetual victims? Possibly. But may they not also be victims of long-duration variable schedules? If you get into a relationship with someone who is fascinating, charming, sexy, fun, and attentive, and then gradually the person becomes more disagreeable, even abusive, though still showing you the good side now and then, you will live for those increasingly rare moments when you are getting all those wonderful reinforcers: the fascinating, charming, sexy, and fun attentiveness. And paradoxically from a commonsense viewpoint, though obviously from the training viewpoint, the rarer and more unpredictable those moments become, the more powerful will be their effect as reinforcers, and the longer your basic behavior will be maintained. Furthermore, it is easy to see why someone once in this kind of relationship might seek it out again. A relationship with a normal person who is decent and friendly most of the time might seem to lack the kick of that rare, longed-for, and thus doubly intense reinforcer.

Look at it from the manipulator's point of view: I can have her/him eating out of my hand, and doing whatever I want, for my comfort and convenience solely, as long as I give her/him what she/he wants . . . once in a while. That's one way pimps keep their whores in line. It's a powerful fix, all right, but once the victim appreciates that the intensity of the "charm" is at least partly due to the nature of the reinforcement schedule, he or she can usually walk quietly away from this kind of relationship and look for something else.

Exceptions to Variable Reinforcement

The one circumstance when one should not go to a variable schedule once the behavior has been learned is when the behavior involves solving some kind of puzzle or test. In advanced obedience training, dogs are asked to select from a group of miscellaneous objects the single object their owner had handled and scented. It is necessary to tell the dog each time that it has selected correctly, so it will know what to do next time. In discrimination tests—identifying the higher of two sounds, let us say—the subject must be reinforced for each correct response so that it continues to be informed as to what question it is being asked. (A conditioned reinforcer will do, of course.) When we play with crossword or jigsaw puzzles, we get reinforced for correct guesses because those are the only ones that "fit." In doing a jigsaw puzzle, if you could put several pieces in each hole, you would not get the positive reinforcer for the right choice, which is necessary feedback in most choice-trial situations.

Long-Duration Behaviors

In addition to variable schedules, one can also establish fixed schedules of reinforcement, in which the subject must work for a predetermined length of time or accomplish a predetermined number of behaviors for each reinforcement. For example, I could arrange for a dolphin to jump six times in a row by reinforcing every sixth jump; soon I would be getting a routine series of six. The trouble with fixed schedules is that the early responses in the series are never reinforced, so they tend to dwindle down to some minimal effort. With the jumping dolphin, in due course all the jumps but the last one, the one that is actually reinforced, would get smaller. This dwindling effect of fixed schedules is probably a factor in many human tasks—factory assembly lines, for example. It is necessary to work for a certain length of time in order to get reinforced, but since the reinforcement is on a fixed schedule, regardless of quality of performance, the subject quite naturally is motivated to do the least amount of work possible to still stay in the game and may perform especially poorly at the start of the work period. Payday on Friday is a fixed reinforcement leading directly to Blue Monday. With the dolphins, occasional random reinforcements for the first or second jump as well as the sixth will help maintain behavior. With people, various kinds of incentive bonuses or other reinforcers (awards, for example) tied directly to quality and quantity of production, and arriving out of synchrony with the usual reinforcement, can be effective.

Using either fixed or variable schedules, extremely long sequences of behavior can be trained. A baby chick can be induced to peck a button a hundred times or more for each grain of corn. For humans there are many examples of delayed gratification. One psychologist jokes that the longest schedule of unreinforced behavior in human existence is graduate school.

In extremely long schedules there is sometimes a point of no return. For the baby chick that point is metabolic; when the chick expends more energy pecking than it can get back from the grain of corn it receives, the behavior tends to die down—the benefits of the job have fallen so low that it simply isn't worth doing. This of course often happens with people as well.

Another phenomenon occurs on very long schedules: slow starts. The chick pecks away at a steady rate once it gets started, because each peck brings it nearer to reinforcement, but researchers have noted that a chick tends to "put off" starting for longer periods as the schedule of reinforcement gets longer.

This is sometimes called delayed start of long-duration behavior, and it's a very familiar aspect of human life. On any long task, from doing the income taxes to cleaning out the garage, one can think of endless reasons for not starting now. Writing, even sometimes just the writing of a letter, is a long-duration behavior. Once it gets started, things usually roll along fairly well, but, oh! it's so hard to make oneself sit down and begin. James Thurber found it so difficult to start an article that he sometimes fooled his wife (who was understandably anxious for him to write articles since that was how the rent got paid) by lying on a couch in his study all morning reading a book in one hand while tapping the typewriter keys at random with the other. The delayed-start phenomenon outweighed the prospect of eventual positive reinforcement of money; and the sham typing at least staved off the negative reinforcer of wifely reproaches.

One way to overcome the slow-start phenomenon is to introduce some reinforcer just for getting started, just as I sporadically reinforced my dolphins for the first or second jump in a six-jump series. I have used this technique effectively in self-training. For some years I went to graduate school one or two nights a week, a long business involving three hours of class and an hour on the subway each way. It was always a huge temptation, as five o'clock rolled around, not to go. But then I found that if I broke down the journey, the first part of the task, into five steps—walking to the subway, catching the train, changing to the next train, getting the bus to the university, and finally, climbing the stairs to the classroom—and reinforced each of these initial behaviors by consuming a small square of chocolate, which I like but normally never eat, at the completion of each step, I was at least able to get myself out of the house, and in a few weeks was able to get all the way to class without either the chocolate or the internal struggle.

Superstitious Behavior: Accidental Reinforcement

Reinforcement occurs all the time in real life, often by coincidence. A biologist studying hawks noticed that if a hawk caught a mouse under a particular bush, it would check out that bush every day for a week or so thereafter; the probability that it would fly over that particular spot had been strongly reinforced. Find a twenty-dollar bill in a trash basket, and I defy you to walk past that trash basket the next day without looking it over closely.

Accidental reinforcement was beneficial to the hawk; in fact, animal behavior in general might be said to have evolved so as to enable each species to benefit from whatever reinforcement occurs. However, accidental pairings also occur, and these can still have a strong effect on behavior. When the behavior is in fact un-related to the consequence, but the subject still exhibits the be-havior as if it were required for earning a reinforcer, scientists call it superstitious behavior. An example is pencil chewing. If, while taking an exam, you happen to put your pencil in your mouth and just then the right answer or a good idea occurs to you, the reinforcer may affect the behavior; good ideas occur during pencil chewing, so pencil chewing is reinforced. When I was in college, I didn't own a pencil that wasn't covered with teeth marks—on really tough exams I sometimes bit pencils right in two. I even felt sure that pencil chewing helped me to think; of course it didn't, it was just accidentally conditioned behavior.

The same goes for wearing a particular garment or going through a ritual when you are about to engage in a task. I have seen one baseball pitcher who goes through a nine-step chain of behavior every time he gets ready to pitch the ball: touch cap, touch ball to glove, push cap forward, wipe ear, push cap back, scuff foot, and so on. In a tight moment he may go through all nine steps twice, never varying the order. The sequence goes by quite fast—announcers never comment on it—and yet it is a very elaborate piece of superstitious behavior.

Superstitious behavior often crops up in training animals. The animal may be responding to criteria you had no intention of es-tablishing but that were accidentally reinforced often enough to become conditioned. For example, the animal may behave as if it has to be in a particular place or facing or sitting a certain way to earn reinforcement. When you want it to work in a new place or face another way, suddenly the behavior mysteriously breaks down, and figuring out why may take some doing. It is wise, therefore, once a behavior has been at least partially trained, to introduce variations in all the circumstances that do not matter to you, lest some accidental conditioning develops that might get in your way later.

Above all, watch out for the development of accidental pat-terns of timing. Both animals and people have a very clear sense of time intervals. I was once quite convinced that I had trained two porpoises to jump on command (a hand signal from me) until a visiting scientist with a stopwatch informed me that they were jumping every twenty-nine seconds. Sure enough, with or without my command, they jumped every twenty-nine seconds. I had become accidentally conditioned to give the command with great regularity, and they had picked up on that instead of on the information I thought they were using.

Many traditional animal trainers are absolutely riddled with superstitious thinking and behavior. I have had some tell me that dolphins prefer people to wear white, that you have to hit mules, that bears don't like women, and so on. And people trainers can be just as bad, believing you have to yell at fifth-graders, for example, or that punishment is needed to create respect. Such trainers are at the mercy of tradition; they have to train the same way every time because they can't separate the methods that are working from methods that are merely superstitious. This failing or confusion crops up in many professions—education, engineering, the military, and perhaps particularly in the medical profession. It is appalling how many things are done to patients not because they are curative but simply because that's the way it's always been done or that's what everyone does nowadays. Anyone who has ever been a patient in a hospital can think of half a dozen examples of unnecessary acts that amounted to nothing more than superstitious behavior.

Interestingly enough, superstitious behavior does not always go away if you merely point out its ineffectiveness; strongly conditioned, it may accordingly be strongly defended. Attack a doctor for his or her habitual use of a nonhelpful or even harmful treatment, and you will be attacked right back—in spades; as I'm sure that pitcher with the nine-step superstitious windup would resist fiercely anyone ordering him to play ball without, say, wearing the cap he touches four times in the sequence.

One way you can get rid of superstitious behavior in yourself, however, is to become aware that it has no relation to reinforcement. My son Ted is a banker whose hobby is competitive fencing. He fits in practice bouts two or three times a week and often travels to tournaments on weekends. One day, facing a stiff competitor, he felt downcast because he had left his favorite blade at home. He lost the match. Then he realized that feeling downcast was probably far more damaging to his performance than the blade he used, and, in fact, that having a "favorite" blade was superstitious behavior.

Ted set out to eliminate every superstitious behavior he could identify related to fencing. He discovered many in his repertoire, from attachment to certain articles of clothing to inner convictions that his game might be affected by a bad night's sleep, an argument, or even by running out of fruit juice at a tournament. Systematically examining each of these circumstances, he eliminated his dependencies one by one as he recognized them as superstitious behavior. Consequently, he now enters each match relaxed and confident, even if the previous hours have been a nightmare of missed trains, lost gear, and battles with taxi drivers, and even if he is fencing with a borrowed blade in a practice uniform with mismatched socks.

What Can You Do with Positive Reinforcement?

Here are some things people I know have done with positive reinforcement:

- Judy, a designer, took a weekly painting class at night at a nearby university to keep her hand in; most of the twenty other people in the class were also designers or commercial artists. The teacher assigned weekly homework, which many of the busy professionals did not bother to complete. The teacher habitually harangued the class for ten minutes or more over the poor showing of homework assignments. Tired of being scolded, Judy suggested he reinforce the ones who did bring in assignments instead of heckling those who didn't. He did so, reinforcing his pupils with public praise of each completed assignment. By the third week, the teacher not only had a happier class, he had raised the number of homeworkers from about a third of the class to nearly three-quarters.

- Shannon, a college student, visited the home of some friends and walked in on a scene. Four adults were trying, unsuccessfully and at some risk to themselves, to restrain the household German shepherd so the dog's infected ear could be medicated. Shannon, not a dog lover particularly but a student of positive reinforcement, got some cheese from the refrigerator and in five minutes trained the dog to hold still while she medicated his ear single-handed.

- A young woman married a man who turned out to be very bossy and demanding. Worse yet, his father, who lived with them, was equally given to ordering his daughter-in-law about. It was the girl's mother who told me this story. On her first visit she was horrified at what her daughter was going through. "Don't worry, Mother," the daughter said, "wait and see." The daughter formed a practice of responding minimally to commands and harsh remarks, while reinforcing with approval and affection any tendency by either man to be pleasant or thoughtful. In a year she had turned them into decent human beings. Now they greet her with smiles when she comes home and leap up—both of them—to help with the groceries.

- An urban eighth-grader liked to take her dog for walks on weekends in the country, but the dog often ran off too far and refused to come back when called, especially when it was time to go home. One weekend the girl started making a huge fuss over the dog—praise, patting, baby talk, hugs, the works—whenever, in running about, it came up to her unbidden. When it was time to go home, she called and the dog came gladly. The huge welcome apparently outweighed, as a reinforcer, the dog's usual prolongation of freedom. It never gave trouble on country walks again.

- A junior executive with a monster of a boss decided which parts of his job might be reinforcing to the boss— bringing papers to be signed, for example—and timed as many as possible to coincide with periods when the boss was not in a rage. The boss eased up and in due course actually started telling jokes.

- Some people develop very special reinforcers that others will go out of their way to earn. Annette, a suburban housewife whose children are grown, might be rather isolated were it not for her network of friends who phone weekly or even more often to share their news. These are not necessarily neighbors or relatives; many are busy professional women who live far away. I am one. Why do we all call Annette? If you have bad news—you've got the flu, or the IRS is going to audit you, or the baby-sitter moved to Cleveland—Annette gives sympathy and advice; but so would any friend. It is in the area of good news that Annette offers unusual reinforcers. Tell her the bank approved your loan, and she does more than say "That's great!" She points out exactly what you did to earn and deserve the good news. "You see?" Annette might respond. "Remember how hard you worked to get a good credit rating? Remember all the trouble you went to with the phone company, and getting an air-travel card? Now it pays off for you; you're recognized as a good businesswoman. But you had to make the right moves first, and you did. I'm really proud of you." Wow! That's more than approval, that is reinforcement—and for past efforts that at the time may have seemed to be merely tribulations. Annette takes good news out of the "good luck" category and turns it into an opportunity for reinforcement. That certainly reinforces one's inclination to call Annette.

Organized Reinforcement

Sales meetings, booster clubs, Dale Carnegie courses, Weight Watchers—in fact, most organizations that teach self-improvement in groups—rely heavily on the effects of reinforcement by the group upon individuals. Applause, medals, awards ceremonies, and other forms of group recognition are powerful reinforcers, sometimes quite imaginatively used. One IBM sales manager, wishing to reinforce his sales team for a good year, hired a football stadium; threw a big party for the employees, senior executives, and all their families; and had his sales force run through the players' tunnel onto the field while their names were flashed on the scoreboard, to the cheers of all assembled.

I went through Werner Erhard's "est" course, a program with overtones of hucksterism but that, from a training standpoint, I found to be an ingenious and often brilliant application of shaping and reinforcement The program was called, rightly I think, the Training. The leader was called the Trainer. The shaping goal was improved self-awareness, and the principal reinforcer was not the Trainer's responses but the nonverbal behavior of the whole group

To develop group behavior as a reinforcer, the 250 people in the group were told to applaud after every speaker, whether they felt like applauding or not Thus from the beginning the shy were encouraged, the bold rewarded, and all contributions, whether insightful or inane, were acknowledged by the group.

At first the applause was dutiful and no more. Soon it became genuinely communicative—not of degrees of enjoyment, as in the theater, but of shades of feeling and meaning. For example, there was in my training class, as I expect there is in every est group, an argumentative man who frequently took issue with what the Trainer said. When this happened for the third or fourth time, the Trainer started arguing back. Now, it was apparent to all that from a logical standpoint, the argumentative man was perfectly correct. But as the argument wore on and on, no one else in the room cared who was right. All 249 of us just wished he'd shut up and sit down.

The rules of the game—shaping rules, really—did not permit us to protest or to tell him to shut up. But gradually the massive silence of the group percolated into his awareness. We watched him realize that no one cared if he was right. Maybe being right was not the only game in town. Slowly he sputtered into silence and sat down. The group instantly erupted in a huge burst of applause, expressive of sympathy and understanding as well as of hearty relief—a very powerful positive reinforcer of the illumination the arguer had just received.

This kind of training occurrence, in which the important events are behavioral and thus nonverbal, is often maddeningly difficult to explain to an outsider. Erhard, like a Zen teacher, often resorts to aphorisms; in the case of the arguer described above, the est saying is "When you're right, that's what you get to be: right." That is, not necessarily loved, or anything else nice: just right. If I were to quote that aphorism at a party when somebody is being bombastic, another est graduate might laugh—and indeed, any good modern trainer might laugh—but most hearers might assume I was moronic or drunk. Good training insights do not necessarily lend themselves to verbal explanation.

Reinforcing Yourself

One possible application of reinforcement training is reinforcing yourself. This is something we often neglect to do, partly because it doesn't occur to us, and partly because we tend to demand a lot more of ourselves than we would of others. As a minister I know puts it, "Few of us have such low standards that it's easy to live up to them." As a result we often go for days at a time without letup, going from task to task to task unnoticed and unthanked even by ourselves. Quite aside from reinforcing oneself for some habit change or new skill, a certain amount of reinforcement is desirable just for surviving daily life; deprivation of reinforcement is one factor, I think, in states of anxiety and depression.

You can reinforce yourself in healthful ways—with an hour off, a walk, a talk with friends, or a good book; or in unhealthful ways—with cigarettes, whiskey, fattening food, drugs, late nights, and so on. I like performer Ruth Gordon's suggestion: "An actor has to have compliments. If I go long enough without getting a compliment, I compliment myself, and that's just as good because at least then I know it's sincere."

2

Shaping: Developing Super Performance Without Strain or Pain

What Is Shaping?

Reinforcing behavior that is already occurring so that it occurs more often is all very well, but how do trainers get their subjects to do things that would probably never occur by chance? How do you get a dog to turn back flips or a dolphin to jump through a hoop?

Dogs flipping, dolphins jumping through hoops, or people throwing basketballs through hoops, for that matter, are developed by shaping. Shaping consists of taking a very small tendency in the right direction and shifting it, one small step at a time, toward an ultimate goal. The laboratory jargon for the process is "successive approximation."

Shaping is possible because the behavior of living things is variable. Whatever a creature does, it will do it with more vigor at some times than at others, in different directions, and so on. No matter how elaborate or difficult the ultimate behavior you wish to shape, you can always, by establishing a series of intermediate goals, find some behavior presently occurring to use as a first step. For example, suppose I decided to train a chicken to "dance." I might begin by watching the chicken moving around as chickens do and reinforcing it every time it happened to move to the left. Soon my first goal would be reached: the chicken would be moving to the left quite often—and, being variable, sometimes a little and sometimes a lot. Now I might selectively reinforce only the stronger movements to the left—turning a quarter circle, say. When these responses predominated, natural variability would again ensure that while some turns were less than a quarter circle, some would be more like half a circle. I could raise my criteria, set a new goal, and start selecting for half-circle turns or better. With the chicken shaped to make several full turns at high speed per reinforcement, I might consider that I'd reached my end goal, a dancing chicken.

We are all quite accustomed to shaping and being shaped. In an informal way much of childrearing is a shaping process. The training of any physical skill, from tennis to typing, consists largely of shaping. We are also shaping when we try to change our own behavior—to quit smoking, say, or to be less shy, or to handle money better.

Our success or failure in shaping a behavior, in ourselves or in others, ultimately depends *not* upon our shaping expertise but upon our persistence. *New York Times* music critic Harold Schonberg wrote of a European conductor who was not really a good conductor but who made fabulous music by keeping his orchestra in rehearsal for each concert for a full year. Most of us can acquire at least some proficiency at almost anything, if we just put enough time into it.

But that's boring. Don't we always want to learn new skills—skiing, piano playing, whatever—as fast as possible? Of course we do, and that's where *good* shaping comes in. Further, don't we prefer to avoid or minimize repetition? Yes again. Of course, some physical skills require repetition, because muscles "learn" slowly and must be put through the motions repeatedly before the motions come easily. Even so, a well-planned shaping program can minimize the required drilling and can make every moment of practice count, thus speeding up progress tremendously. And finally, in sports, music, and other creative endeavors, you may want to develop not only reliable performance but as good a performance as you or the one you're training can possibly give. In that case, correct use of the laws governing shaping may be crucial.

Methods Versus Principles

There are two aspects to shaping: the methods—that is, the behaviors that are to be developed and the sequence of steps used to develop them—and the principles, or rules governing how, when, and why those behaviors are reinforced.

Most trainers, most books about training, and most teachers of training are concerned almost entirely with method. "Place your hands on the golf club as in the drawing"; "Line up your rifle sights before you aim at the target"; "Never lean into the mountain"; "Beat the eggs with a wire whisk in a clockwise direction." This is fine. Such methods usually have been developed over many years, by many people, through trial and error, so they do work. It's probably true that you'll sit on a horse more securely if you keep your heels down, or that your golf ball will go farther if you shape a good follow-through into your swing. If you are interested in learning a particular skill, I would strongly urge that you find out as much as possible about the established methods of accomplishing the behaviors that that skill involves, through books, teachers, or coaches and through watching or studying others.

On the other side of shaping, however, are the principles, the rules that control such matters as when to press on and when to let up; how to escalate your criteria most efficiently; what to do when you run into trouble; above all, perhaps, when to quit. These questions are generally left to the intuition and experience of trainers or coaches, or to chance or luck. Yet it is the successful application of such principles that makes the difference between an adequate teacher and a great one, and between shaping that is happy, fast, and successful and shaping that is frustrating, slow, boring, and disagreeable. It's good shaping, not just good methods, that makes training effective.

The Ten Laws of Shaping

There are ten rules that govern shaping, as I see it. Some come straight from the psychology labs and have been demonstrated experimentally. Others have not even been the subject of formal study, so far as I know, but can be recognized as inherently valid by anyone who has done a lot of shaping: You always know (usually an instant too late) when you've broken one. I'll list the rules here, then discuss each one at some length:

1. Raise criteria in increments small enough that the subject always has a realistic chance for reinforcement.
2. Train one aspect of any particular behavior at a time; don't try to shape for two criteria simultaneously.
3. During shaping, put the current level of response onto a variable schedule of reinforcement before adding or raising the criteria.
4. When introducing a new criterion, or aspect of the behavioral skill, temporarily relax the old ones.
5. Stay ahead of your subject: Plan your shaping program completely so that if the subject makes sudden progress, you are aware of what to reinforce next.
6. Don't change trainers in midstream; you can have several trainers per trainee, but stick to one shaper per behavior.
7. If one shaping procedure is not eliciting progress, find another; there are as many ways to get behavior as there are trainers to think them up.
8. Don't interrupt a training session gratuitously; that constitutes a punishment.

9. If behavior deteriorates, "go back to kindergarten"; quickly review the whole shaping process with a series of easily earned reinforcers.

10. End each session on a high note, if possible, but in any case quit while you're ahead.

DISCUSSION

1. Raise criteria in increments small enough that the subject always has a realistic chance of reinforcement.

In practice this means that when you increase demands or raise a criterion for reinforcement, you should do so within the range the subject is already achieving. If your horse clears two-foot jumps, sometimes with a foot to spare, you could start raising some jumps to two and a half feet. Raising them all to three feet would be asking for trouble: The animal is capable of this but is not offering it regularly yet. And raising the jumps to three and a half feet would be courting disaster.

How fast you raise the criteria is *not* a function of the subject's actual ability, now or in the future; never mind if the horse is a big leggy creature potentially capable of jumping eight feet, or if it habitually hops over four-foot pasture fences. How fast you can raise the criteria is a function of how well you are communicating through your shaping procedure what your rules are for gaining reinforcement.

Every time you raise a criterion, you are changing the rules. The subject has to be given the opportunity to discover that though the rules have changed, reinforcers can easily continue to be earned by an increase in exertion (and also, in some cases, that performing at the old level no longer works). This can be learned only by experiencing reinforcement at the new level.

If you raise the criteria so high that the subject has to exert itself far beyond anything it has previously done *for you*—regardless of what it does or doesn't do on its own time—you are taking a big risk. The behavior may break down. A jumper might learn bad habits, such as balking or knocking down jumps, habits that will be very time-consuming to eliminate. The fastest way to shape behavior—sometimes the only way—is to raise the criteria at whatever interval it takes to make it *easy* for the subject to improve steadily. Constant progress, even if only inch by inch, will get you to your ultimate goal much faster than trying to force rapid progress at the risk of losing good performance altogether.

I once saw a father make a serious error in this regard. Because his teenage son was doing very badly in school, he confiscated the youth's beloved motorcycle until his grades improved. The boy did work harder, and his grades did improve, from Fs and Ds to Ds and Cs. Instead of reinforcing this progress, however, the father said that the grades had not improved *enough* and continued to withhold bike privileges. This escalation of the criteria was too big a jump; the boy stopped working altogether. He furthermore became very mistrustful.

2. *Train one aspect of any particular behavior at a time; don't try to shape for two criteria simultaneously.*

I don't mean that you can't be working on many different behaviors over the same period of time. Of course you can. In any sort of lesson we might work on form for a while and then on speed— in tennis, on the backhand, then the forehand, then on footwork, and so on. It relieves monotony. Good teachers vary the work all the time, leaving one task as soon as some progress has been made and going on to another.

While you are working on a given behavior, however, you should work on one criterion at a time, and only that one. If I were training a dolphin to splash and I were to withhold reinforcer one time because the splash was not big enough and the next time because it was in the wrong direction, the animal would have no way of deciphering what I wanted from it. One reinforcement cannot convey two pieces of information: I should shape for size of splash until satisfied with that and then shape for direction of splash, whatever the size, until that, too, is learned; only when both criteria are established could I require both to be obeyed.

Rule 2 has a lot of practical applications. If the task can be broken down into separate components, which are then shaped separately, the learning will go much faster.

Take learning to putt. Putting a golf ball depends on sending it the right distance—not short of the cup and not past it or over it—and sending it in the right direction, not to one side of the cup or the other. If I were going to teach myself to putt, I would practice these separately. Perhaps I would put a piece of tape on the grass, several feet long, and practice hitting the ball just across the tape first from two feet, then four, six, and ten feet, and so on. I might also make a circle of tape, and practice aiming at it from a fixed distance, gradually reducing the circle's size, until I could hit a very small target reliably. Only when I was satisfied with my skills for both distance and direction would I combine them, setting up a large target size and varying the distance, then reducing the target size and varying the distance again until I could hit a small target at many distances. I would then add more criteria, one at a time, such as putting uphill.

This might make me an excellent or even a superb putter, depending on my dedication and the upper limits of my hand-eye coordination. It would certainly, within my capacity, make me a reliable putter. What I am suggesting is that any golfer could improve more in a few weekends following such a single-task shaping program than in a whole summer of random putting practice, hoping willy-nilly to get both the correct distance and the right direction on every shot.

Often when we seem to show no progress in a skill, no matter how much we practice, it is because we are trying to improve two or more things at once. Practice is not shaping. Repetition, by itself, may ingrain mistakes just as easily as improvements. One needs to think: Does this behavior have more than one attribute? Is there some way to break it down and work on different criteria separa... ...n you address both of these questions, many problems ... ...lves.

3. During shaping, put the current level of response onto a variable schedule of reinforcement before adding or raising the criteria.

Many people initially object to the idea of using positive reinforcers in training because they imagine that they will forever have to hand out treats to get good behavior. But the opposite is true. Training with reinforcement actually frees you from the need for constant vigilance over the behavior, because of the power of variable schedules.

A variable schedule of reinforcement simply means that sometimes you reinforce a behavior and sometimes you don't. Often when we are teaching the behavior, we use a *fixed* schedule of reinforcement; that is, we reinforce every adequate behavior. But when we are just maintaining a behavior, we reinforce very occasionally, using a sporadic or intermittent schedule. For example, once a pattern of chore sharing has been established, your roommate or spouse may stop at the dry cleaners on the way home without being reinforced each time; but you might express thanks for an extra trip made when you are ill or the weather is bad.

When we train with aversives, however—and that's the way most of us began—we are usually taught that it is vital to correct every mistake or misbehavior. When errors are not corrected, the behavior breaks down. Many dogs are well behaved on the leash, when they might get jerked, but they are highly unreliable as soon as they are off leash and out of reach. When out with their friends, many teenagers do things that they wouldn't dream of doing in their parents' presence. This can happen because the subject is fully aware that punishment is unavailable—when the cat's away, the mice will play—but it can also happen as a side effect of training with aversives. Since the message in a punisher is "Don't do *that*," the absence of the aversive sends the message, "*That* is okay now."

With positive reinforcement, on the other hand, not only is it *not* necessary to reinforce every correct response for a lifetime, but it is crucial to the learning process to skip an occasional reinforcer. Why?

The heart of the shaping procedure consists of selectively reinforcing some responses rather than others, so that the response improves, little by little, until it reaches a new goal. All behavior is variable; when you skip an expected reinforcer, the next behavior is likely to be somewhat different. Thus the skipped reinforcer enables you to select stronger or better responses. That's sometimes called a "differential" or "selective" schedule of reinforcement; you are choosing to reinforce only some kinds of responses: those that meet, say, the requirement of being faster or longer, or facing left but not right.

But to an inexperienced learner who until now has been earning reinforcers pretty predictably, skipping reinforcers can be a shock. Your puppy sits, you click and treat for the sit, the puppy sits faster and more and more gleefully—"Look! I'm *sitting*! Click me!" And now suddenly, some sits don't work! If your puppy has not learned to withstand an occasional skipped reinforcer, it may well quit in despair or go back to a weaker or slower response. While this step is not mentioned in the learning textbooks, in practice it is useful, if you are working with a new and inexperienced learner, to deliberately teach your trainee to tolerate small variations in the reinforcement schedule, before you begin to select for bigger or better responses. Your subject has to be able to tolerate an occasional failure per se, without stopping the behavior altogether. Or, technically speaking, you need to establish an intermittent schedule of reinforcement before starting to hold out for improved performance through a differential schedule of reinforcement.

In dog training seminars in the 1990s I labeled this type of variable schedule—a brief use of intermittent reinforcement—"twofers," Broadway slang for two theater tickets for the price of one. Let the dog do it twice—two bumps of the target with its nose, say—for one click or treat. Learning to tolerate an intermittent schedule makes the behavior—and other subsequent behaviors—more resistant to extinction.

There's another benefit to this brief use of an intermittent schedule during the learning phase. When your subject is able to tolerate the occasional skipped reinforcer, and you let a previously adequate response go by without a reinforcer, the learner is likely not only to repeat the behavior but to repeat it with more vigor: "Hey! I did it, didn't you see me? Look! I'm doing it again!" This intensified behavior—called an extinction burst—enables you to move more rapidly toward your goal behavior. A skilled shaper may even omit reinforcers specifically in order to provoke a varied or more vigorous response. Dog behaviorist Gary Wilkes calls this "surfing the extinction bursts."

Once the subject has learned that a skipped reinforcer does not mean the behavior was wrong but simply that one might need to try again, the shaping flows from continuous reinforcement (as a new behavior surfaces) to differential reinforcement (as we select for better form, longer duration, faster speed, shorter latencies, and so on) and then back to continuous reinforcement (whenever the behavior is "perfect" or, in laboratory terms, "meets criteria"). Deliberate use of intermittent reinforcement is no longer necessary because the learner already tolerates variable schedules.

Ultimately, when the behavior is satisfactory in all respects, it usually becomes part of a repertoire. One requires this behavior as a part of other, more complex behaviors; good form, speed, distance, and so on are blended into a whole—the race, the job, the day's activities—and that whole becomes the behavior that is reinforced. With this behavior you are now back to an intermittent or maintenance schedule, just the sporadic clicks or "Thanks!" that serve to keep things running smoothly. The high rate of positive reinforcement, the flood of clicks and treats that you may have used in the beginning, can now be saved for learning some other new behavior.

4. When introducing a new criterion or aspect of the behavioral skill, temporarily relax the old ones.

Suppose you're learning to play squash, and you've been working successfully on aim—sending the ball where you want it to go. Now you'd like to work on speed, but when you hit hard, the ball goes every which way. Forget about aim for a while and just slam the ball. When you have achieved some control over the speed of the ball, your aim will come back very quickly.

What is once learned is not forgotten, but under the pressure of assimilating new skill levels, old well-learned behavior some-times falls apart temporarily. I once saw a conductor, during the first dress rehearsal of an opera, having a tantrum because the singers in the chorus were making one musical mistake after another; they seemed virtually to have forgotten all their hard-learned vocal accomplishment. But they were, for the first time, wearing heavy costumes, standing on ladders, being required to move about as they sang: Getting used to new requirements tem-porarily interfered with previously learned behavior. By the end of the rehearsal, the musical learning reappeared, without coach-ing. Dolphin trainers call this the "new tank syndrome." When you move a dolphin to a new tank, you have to expect that it will "forget" all it knows until the new stimuli are assimilated. It is im-portant to realize that berating yourself or others for mistakes in past-learned behavior under new circumstances is bad training. The mistakes will usually clear up by themselves shortly, but rep-rimands cause upset and sometimes tend to draw attention to the mistakes so they *don't* go away.

5. Stay ahead of your subject.

Plan your shaping program so that if your subject makes a sud-den leap forward, you will know what to reinforce next. I once spent two days shaping a newly captured dolphin to jump over a bar a few inches above the water surface. When the behavior was well established, I raised the bar another few inches; the animal jumped immediately, and so easily that I shortly raised the bar again and by a bigger increment; in fifteen minutes this novice animal was jumping eight feet.

A shaping "breakthrough" of this sort can happen at any time. We see the phenomenon in people, of course, and in many species of intelligent animals. I believe it's an example of insight

The subject suddenly realizes the point of what it's being asked to do (in this case, to jump much higher) and goes out and does it. Killer whales are famous for anticipating shaping. Their trainers all have the same joke: You don't have to train killer whales, you just write the behavior on a blackboard and hang it in the water, and the whales will follow the script.

Where trainers can run into trouble is if they are not ready for sudden improvement. If you as trainer are going from A to B, and the subject suddenly does B perfectly in two reinforcements, you'd better have in mind steps C and D, or you will have nothing further to reinforce.

Breakthroughs often seem to be extremely exciting for the subject; even animals appear to enjoy a kind of "Aha!" experience and often rush about evincing elation. A breakthrough is thus a golden opportunity to make a lot of progress in a hurry. To be unprepared and to hold the subject at a low level of performance just because you don't know what to do next is at best a waste of time and at worst may discourage or disgust your subject so that it becomes less willing to work in the future.

Except under the very best of circumstances, our whole school system seems to be set up to prevent children from learning at their own rate—to penalize not only the slow learners, who don't get the time to learn, but the fast learners, who don't get additional reinforcement when quick thinking moves them ahead. If you understand in a flash what your math teacher is talking about, your reward may be to writhe in boredom for hours, even weeks, while everyone else learns by inches. No wonder street life looks like more fun for the quick ones as well as the slow.

6. Don't change trainers in midstream.

While in the midst of shaping a behavior, you risk major slowdowns if you turn the training over to someone else. No matter how scrupulous one may be in discussing criteria before turning over the job, everyone's standards, reaction times, and expectations of progress are slightly different, and the net effect for the subject is to lose reinforcers until those differences can be accommodated. In a way it's another example of "new tank syndrome."

Of course one trainee may have many different teachers—we have no trouble when one trainer teaches us French, another arithmetic, another football. It is the individual behavior being learned that needs one teacher at a time. During the shaping, or half-learned, stages, consistency of the gradually escalating criteria is best maintained by keeping the shaping of a given behavior in one person's hands. So if, say, you have two children and one dog, and both kids want to teach the dog tricks, let them; but let them each work on separate tricks and spare the poor dog a lot of confusion.

Those who want to learn will learn under the worst of circumstances. One of the by now well-known "ape language" experiments, in which apes are taught vocabularies in American Sign Language and other codes, took place at Columbia University and involved a baby chimpanzee named Nim Chimpsky Because of budgetary and other problems, the poor creature had more than one hundred "teachers" of signing in a three-year period. The students and experimenters were disappointed that Nim showed no firm evidence of real "language." That is, he apparently never made sentences. But he did learn to recognize and understand more than three hundred signs—nouns, verbs, and so on—which, under the circumstances, I think is amazing. And so some children go from school to school and through the hands of endless processions of substitute teachers and still learn. But there are better ways.

The one time that you should consider changing trainers in midshaping is, of course, when the training is going nowhere. If little or no learning is occurring, you have nothing to lose by switching.

7. *If one shaping procedure is not eliciting progress, try another.*

No matter what the behavior, there are as many ways to shape it as there are trainers to think them up. In teaching children to swim, for example, one wants to get them to be fearless and comfortable about going underwater. As a first step in this shaping task, one teacher may get them blowing bubbles in the water; another may have them put their faces in quickly and out again; a third may get them bobbing up and down until they dare to bob underneath. Any good teacher, seeing that a child is bored by or afraid of one method, will switch to another; the same shaping methods don't work equally well on every individual.

Traditional trainers, such as circus trainers, often fail to grasp this point. Their shaping procedures have been honed over generations and passed down through families—this is the way you train a bear to ride a bicycle, this is the way you train a lion to roar (tweak a few hairs out of its mane, if you want to know). These traditional "recipes" are considered the best ways, and sometimes they are, but they are also often considered the only ways, which is one reason why circus acts tend to look so much alike.

The radio and television star Arthur Godfrey, after doing a show at Sea Life Park, invited me to visit him and his wife at their farm in Virginia to watch the horse training. Godfrey was an excellent rider and trainer himself and owned a number of performing horses. We were watching a horse being trained to bow, or kneel on one knee, by a traditional method involving two men and a lot of ropes and whips; the horse under this method is repeatedly forced onto one knee until it learns to go down voluntarily.

I said it didn't have to be done that way and asserted that I could train a horse to bow without ever touching the animal. (One possibility: Put a red spot on the wall; use food and a marker signal to shape the horse to touch its knee to the spot; then lower the spot gradually to the floor so that to touch it correctly and earn a reinforcer the horse has to kneel.) Godfrey became so angry at this impertinent suggestion—the idea! If there were another way to train a bow, he would know about it—that we had to walk him around the outside of the barn two or three times to cool him off.

It is amazing how tenaciously people will stick to a system that isn't working, or that works badly, convinced somehow that more of the same will get results. Murray Sidman, Ph.D., a pioneering researcher in behavior analysis, maintains that this is the *main* reason why it's important to understand the principles and not just learn recipes. Everyone has a "method." The principles govern what truly works.

8. Don't interrupt a training session gratuitously; that constitutes a punishment.

This doesn't apply to the casual (though meaningful and productive) shaping one might do around the house—praising schoolwork, welcoming homecomers, encouraging children; a reinforcer here and there, with no formality, will do fine. In a more formal situation, however—in giving a lesson, say, or in shaping behavior in an animal—the trainer should keep his or her attention on the training subject or the class until the training period is over. This is more than just good manners or good self-discipline; it is skilled training. When a subject essays to earn reinforcers, it enters into a contract, so to speak, with the trainer. If the trainer starts chatting to some bystander or leaves to answer the telephone or is merely daydreaming, the contract is broken; reinforcement is unavailable through no fault of the trainee. This does more harm than just putting the trainer at risk of missing a good opportunity to reinforce. It may punish some perfectly good behavior that was going on at the time.

Of course if you *want* to rebuke a subject, removing your attention is a good way to do it. Dolphin trainers call this a timeout and use it to correct misbehavior. Picking up the fish bucket and walking away for one minute is one of the few ways one has of saying "No!" or "Wrong!" to a dolphin, and it is usually very effective; one wouldn't think dolphins could look chagrined or act contrite, but they can. Removal of attention is a powerful tool, so don't use it carelessly or unfairly.

9. If a learned behavior deteriorates, review the shaping.

Sometimes a skill or behavior gets rusty or seems to be totally lost. We all know how it feels to try to speak a language or remember a poem or ride a bicycle if we haven't done it in years and years: It feels most unsettling. Sometimes outside circumstances will temporarily eradicate a well-learned behavior—when stage fright, for instance, makes it impossible to give the thoroughly memorized speech, or a bad fall severely affects your rock-climbing skills. Sometimes subsequent learning overlies or contradicts the original learning, so that mix-ups occur—you strive for the Spanish word and come up with the German.

Sometimes the side effects of punishment or other aversive events interfere with unrelated behavior. Attorney and dog fancier Morgan Spector describes an obedience trial in which every single dog that competed shied away from one particular corner of the ring. What aversive lurked there? Only the dogs knew.

Sometimes an apparently well-trained behavior just breaks down, and you never will identify the reason. Your high-scoring competition obedience dog who has never done such a thing before in his life gets up in the middle of the three-minute Long Sit exercise and wanders out of the ring. Who knows why? Who cares why? What is needed is not justification but an effective fix.

The quickest way to correct this kind of deterioration is not to butt at it head-on, insisting that the subject get the whole thing back before you're satisfied or before you reinforce, but to recall the original shaping procedure and go all the way through it very rapidly, reinforcing under the new circumstances (twenty years later, in public, in the rain, whatever) and just reinforcing once or twice at each level. At Sea Life Park we called this "going back to kindergarten," and the technique often brought a poor behavior up to par in ten or fifteen minutes.

Of course we are doing just this whenever we review for an exam or refresh our memories by glancing at a script before going onstage. It is useful to remember that if you can more or less match the original shaping process, reviewing works equally well for physical as for mental skills. And it works with animals as well as people.

10. Quit while you're ahead.

How long should a shaping session run? That depends partly on the attention span of the subject. Cats often seem to get restless after perhaps a dozen reinforcers, so five minutes might be plenty. Dogs and horses can work longer. Human lessons of many sorts are traditionally an hour long, and football practice, graduate seminars, and various other endeavors often go on all day.

When you stop is not nearly as important as what you stop on. You should *always* quit while you're ahead. This is true for whole sessions, but it also applies to stages within a session, when you stop working on one behavior and go on to another. You should move on on a high note—that is, as soon as some progress has been achieved.

The last behavior that was accomplished is the one that will be remembered best; you want to be sure it was a good, reinforceable performance. What happens all too often is that we get three or four good responses—the dog retrieves beautifully, the diver does a one-and-a-half for the first time, the singer gets a difficult passage right—and we are so excited that we want to see it again or to do it again. So we repeat it, or try to, and pretty soon the subject is tired, the behavior gets worse, mistakes crop up, corrections and yelling take place, and we just blew a training session. Amateur riders are always doing this. I detest watching people practice jumping their horses; so often they go past the point when they should have stopped, when the animal was doing well and before the behavior began falling apart.

As a trainer you should force yourself, if necessary, to stop on a good response. It takes guts sometimes. But you may find that in the next session the retrieve, the somersault dive, the solo obbligato is not only as good as the last one of the previous session but noticeably better. At the start of the next session, the performance may actually begin a step beyond where it left off, and then you have just that much more to reinforce.

Shaping behavior is, of course, the opposite of training by drill and repetition. It can produce not only steady progress but absolutely error-free training, and this can go extremely fast; I once halter-broke a pony yearling in fifteen minutes, from start to finish, and permanently, by moving back and forth between five shaping tasks (forward, stop, left, right, and back) while reinforcing progress in each one. Accomplishing such speedy training depends, paradoxically, on your willingness to give up time limits, specific goal setting, and speed of progress itself as a goal. You must instead count simply on your willingness to quit while you're ahead. A Zen phenomenon.

Sometimes you can't end each training session on a high note. Perhaps the students paid for an hour and they want an hour, though a good quitting time was reached earlier. Or perhaps the session really isn't going well enough to provide a high point, but fatigue is soon going to be a problem. In that case it is wise to end the session with some easy, guaranteed way to earn a reinforcer so that the session as a whole is remembered as being reinforcing. Dolphin trainers often end long, demanding sessions with a bit of easy ball playing; riding teachers sometimes use games such as Simon Says or tag. The most inadvisable technique is to introduce new tasks or material late in the session so that it concludes with a series of inadequate and unreinforced behaviors. My piano lessons, as a child, always ended this way; it was very discouraging and I still can't play the piano.

The Training Game

Even if you know and understand the principles of shaping, you can't apply them unless you practice them. Shaping is not a verbal process, it is a nonverbal skill—a flow of interactive behavior through time, like dancing, or making love, or surfing. As such, it can't really be learned by reading or thinking or talking about it. You have to do it.

One easy and fascinating way to develop shaping skills is by playing the Training Game. I use the Training Game in teaching the techniques of training. Many trainers play it for sport; it makes an interesting party game.

You need two people at least: the subject and the trainer. Six is ideal because then every person can experience being both subject and trainer at least once before the group gets tired; but larger groups—a classroom or lecture audience, for example—are feasible, because observing is almost as much fun as participating.

You send the subject out of the room. The rest of the people select a trainer and choose a behavior to be shaped: for example, to write one's name on the blackboard, jump up and down, or stand on a chair. The subject is invited back in and told to move about the room and be active; the trainer reinforces, by blowing on a whistle, movements in the general direction of the desired behavior. I like to make a rule at least for the first few reinforcements that the "animal" has to go back to the doorway after each reinforcer and start anew; it seems to help prevent a tendency of some subjects to just stand still wherever reinforcement was last received. And no talking. Laughter, groans, and other signs of emotion are permitted, but instructions and discussion are out until after the behavior is achieved.

Ordinarily the Training Game goes quite fast. Here's an example: Six of us are playing the game in a friend's living room. Ruth volunteers to be the animal, and it's Anne's turn to be the trainer. Ruth goes out of the room. We all decide that the behavior should be to turn on the lamp on the end table beside the couch.

Ruth is called back in and begins wandering around the room. When she heads in the direction of the lamp, Anne blows the whistle. Ruth goes back to "Start" (the doorway), then moves purposefully to the spot where she was reinforced and stops. No whistle. She waves her hands about. No whistle. She moves off the spot, tentatively, away from the lamp as it happens. Still hearing no whistle, Ruth begins walking around again. When once again she walks toward the lamp, Anne blows the whistle

Ruth returns to the door and then returns to the new spot where she just heard the whistle, but this time she keeps walking forward. Bingo: whistle. Without going back to the door, she walks forward some more and hears the whistle just as she is coming up against the end table. She stops. She bumps the end table. No whistle. She waves her hands around; no whistle. One hand brushes the lampshade, and Anne whistles. Ruth begins touching the lampshade all over—moving it, turning it, rocking it: no whistle. Ruth reaches up underneath the lampshade. Whistle. Ruth reaches underneath the shade again, and, the gesture being very familiar and having a purpose, she executes the purpose and turns on the lamp. Anne whistles and the rest of us applaud.

Things don't always go that smoothly, even with simple, familiar behaviors. Anne, as it turned out, made a good training decision when she withheld reinforcement as Ruth moved from the spot where she'd first been reinforced, but in the wrong direction. If, however, Ruth had then moved back to the spot and just stood there, Anne might have been in trouble.

Here's an example of a round of the Training Game that presented more of a problem. I was teaching training in a high school class. Leonard was the animal and Beth the trainer. The behavior was to turn on the ceiling lights with a wall switch.

Leonard came into the room and began moving about, and Beth quickly shaped him to go to the wall where the light switch was. However, Leonard had started out with his hands in his pockets; after several reinforcements for moving about with his hands in his pockets, they were stuck there as if glued. He bumped the wall, he turned and leaned on the wall, he even leaned on the light switch, but the switch seemed to be invisible to him and he never took his hands out of his pockets.

As I watched, I thought that if Leonard could be induced to feel the wall with a hand, he would notice the switch and turn on the light. But how to get those hands out of the pockets? Beth had another idea. She "caught" with the whistle a bent-knees movement while Leonard had his back to the wall and soon had shaped him to rub his back up and down on the wall near the switch. The other students giggled as they realized that by shifting the movement sideways Beth might get Leonard to move the switch with his back, thus meeting the criterion accidentally, if not deliberately. But it was a slow business, and we could see that Leonard was getting frustrated and angry.

"Can I try?" asked Maria. Beth glanced at me for approval, I shrugged, the class seemed to acquiesce, and Maria got out her own whistle. (Acquiring a whistle was the only course requirement.) Maria waved Leonard back to the "Start" position at the door and then moved a chair near the light switch, about a foot out from the wall, sat down on it herself, and nodded to Leonard to begin. He headed briskly for the wall where he had been reinforced so often, passing Maria and apparently ignoring her new position. As he passed her, she stuck out her foot and tripped him.

Leonard's hands flew out of his pockets and against the wall, to break his fall; as his hands hit, the whistle blew. Leonard froze. He looked at Maria. She gazed into the middle distance, to avoid cuing him in any way. Tentatively he began patting the wall; she reinforced that. He patted the wall again, and this time he looked at what he was doing; she reinforced that. Then we all saw Leonard focus abruptly on the light switch. No one breathed. He straightened his spine a little, suddenly full of awareness, and switched on the lights. Tumultuous applause.

Everyone involved in the Training Game, participants and spectators alike, learns from almost every reinforcer. The trainer, first of all, gets to discover what timing is all about. Suppose the subject approaches the light switch, but just as the trainer blows the whistle, the subject turns away. Well, thinks the trainer, I'll catch it next time. But now suppose the subject goes back to the starting point, then hurries toward the switch and whirls away from it. Groan. The trainer has shaped that whirl. And everyone, not just the trainer, sees how crucial it is to get the whistle in a little earlier, while the desired behavior is actually occurring.

The subject gets to discover that in this form of learning, brains don't help. It doesn't matter what you are thinking about; if you just keep moving around, collecting whistle sounds, your body will find out what to do without "your" help. This is an absolutely excruciating experience for brilliant, intellectual people. They tend to freeze when they hear the whistle and to try to analyze what they were doing. That they don't know, and that it doesn't matter that they don't know, is a shocker. A colleague, Sheri Gish, and I once trained psychologist Ronald Schusterman to walk around the room with his hands clenched behind his back for periods of up to a minute—a long time to go without a reinforcer, but he was diligent—until the assembled room agreed that we had the behavior thoroughly established, and burst into applause. (That is the reinforcer for the trainer, incidentally, and it almost always occurs spontaneously.) Ron, who trains many animals in his research, and who had rashly opined that he himself "could not be trained," was unaware that his clenched fists behind his back were now a shaped behavior, not just a subliminal expression of opinion.

What this demonstrates is not some Machiavellian nature of reinforcement training but the hazards in our habitual error of assuming that verbal communication is all-important, and that learning cannot take place without the use of language or at least some verbal consciousness. The experience of nonverbal learning is especially useful for people who do a lot of verbal instructing in their professional lives: teachers, therapists, supervisors. Once you have been the "animal," you can sympathize, even empathize, with any subject that is exhibiting the behavior you are shaping but has not yet *comprehended* what it is supposed to be doing, so that it easily makes mistakes. You can have patience with the animal (or the child or patient) that explodes in frustration and rage when what it had confidently thought was the right thing to do turns out to be no good, a contretemps that can bring human subjects close to tears. And once you have performed nonverbal shaping with adult human subjects in an exercise, you may not be so quick to say in a teaching, coaching, or training situation in real life that the subject (animal, student, whatever) "hates me," or "is deliberately trying to get my goat," or "is stupid," or "must be sick today." It is patently obvious, during this exercise in which everyone is participating by agreement and with a will, that whatever goes wrong is a function of the training, not the trainee.

The illumination this game provides for professionals is part of the fun (and everyone else gets your insights at the same time—you can't hide, but on the other hand you are bathed in amused sympathy). A charm of the game purely as entertainment is that anyone can play it without previous experience. Some people have a wonderful knack for it. In my experience intuitive, creative, intensely emotional people make great shapers, and calm, observant people make great animals—just the opposite of what you might expect. Finally, one has only to look at a roomful of people intent on the shaping going on, with everyone motionless but the subject, and the trainer's whole body and mind focused on the task, to see that this is an experience akin to painting or writing: It is creative work. Except on stage, creativity is rarely shared as a group experience. The Training Game is valuable for that aspect alone.

We played some memorable rounds of the Training Game at Sea Life Park, especially one in which philosopher Gregory Bateson, being the "animal" for some of my dolphin trainers, proved indeed to be impossible to train, not because he stood still and thought but because he offered such an endless variety of responses that the trainer was swamped. Another to me very interesting round of this game occurred following a luncheon of six professional women, mostly unknown to each other and from widely unrelated fields. After two hours of the game, in which a psychotherapist proved to be a marvelous "animal" and a disco dancer a brilliant shaper, we left knowing each other much better and liking each other a good deal, too.

In 1980 I taught an experimental course in training to a group of high school students at the Brearley School in New York City. We played the Training Game in class, and a hard core of half a dozen fiendishly imaginative young women began playing the Training Game at home among themselves, working in pairs usually, and shaping exotic behaviors such as crawling upstairs backward. They had been taught—successfully, in my opinion—to think analytically at the Brearley School, and they correctly did their hard thinking before and after a shaping session and flung themselves into the shaping itself with the normal gusto of sixteen-year-olds. In no time they were shaping parents, using positive reinforcement on teachers, and turning obnoxious siblings into amusing companions by selectively reinforcing desired behavior. I never saw a group, before or since, grasp both the techniques and their possibilities so rapidly.

Shaping Shortcuts: Targeting, Mimicry, and Modeling

Professional trainers use a number of techniques to make shaping go faster. Three that may be of use to you are targeting, mimicry, and modeling.

In targeting, which is widely used in the training of sea lions and other performing animals, you shape the animal to touch its nose to a target—a knob on the end of a pole, say, or often simply the trainer's closed fist. Then, by moving the target around and getting the animal merely to go and touch it, you can elicit all kinds of other behavior, such as climbing stairs, jumping or rearing up, following the trainer, getting into and out of a shipping crate, and so on. We are essentially using targeting when we slap our thighs to coax a dog to us. The movement seems to attract dogs, and when they approach, we reinforce the behavior with petting. Patting the couch to invite someone to sit beside you is a form of targeting. Japanese tourist groups stick together among crowds of much taller people by following a flag held above the crowd by their tour leaders—again, targeting. Flags and banners have traditionally served the same purpose in battle. Targeting has become an important tool in the new field of reinforcement training, or "clicker training," for dogs, horses, and zoo animals.

Mimicry comes naturally to some animals and birds, as well as to people. Young creatures of all sorts learn much of what they need to know by watching and then copying the behavior of their elders. While "learning by observation" is often taken by psychologists as a sign of intelligence in animals—primates being good at it and some other animals poor—I think the presence or absence of this skill in a species is a function of its ecology—that is, of its role in nature—rather than of intelligence per se. Some birds are remarkably good at behavioral mimicry. Titmice in England learned to open milk bottles on doorsteps and drink the cream, a skill that, through mimicry, spread so rapidly through the titmouse population that milk-bottle tops had to be redesigned.

Many dogs are *not* good at learning by observation; when they do what other dogs are doing, it is usually because they are responding to the same stimuli, not because they are mimicking. On the other hand, most cats, which get lower "IQ scores" than dogs from the animal psychologists, are wonderful mimickers. The folk expression "copycat" is no accident. If you teach a trick—ringing the doorbell to be let in, say—to one cat in the household, new or other cats may well learn it with no training from you. Cats will even copy noncats. One evening my daughter spent an hour teaching her poodle to sit on a child's rocking chair and rock it, using chopped ham as the reinforcer. One of the cats was watching. When the lesson was over, the cat, unprompted, got on the chair and rocked it most correctly, looking up for its own share of chopped ham, which it most certainly had earned.

I think this strong tendency to mimic explains why cats get stuck in trees. Climbing up comes more or less automatically: It is, as biologists say, "hard-wired." The claws stick out and the cat runs up the tree. To get down, however, the cat has to descend backward, so that its down-curved claws can still operate, and this appears to be a learned, or "soft-wired," skill. I can testify to this because I have personally (in the middle of the night, and on top of a ladder) shaped a cat to come down a tree backward. I did so in order to spare myself the mournful yowls of a stuck cat in the future, and indeed the cat stayed shaped—it never got stuck again (though it continued to climb trees). I think in nature cats learn how to turn around and descend backward from watching their mothers as they climb trees together, but because we take them from their mothers at such a tender age—six to eight weeks—this opportunity for copycatting is lost.

Dolphins have a strong tendency to mimic one another, which facilitates training. To get several dolphins doing the same thing you shape the behavior in one, then reinforce the others for any attempt to copy. In captivity baby dolphins often learn the adults' tricks long before they themselves are old enough for fish rewards, and many oceanariums have had the experience of "understudies," animals on the sidelines that watch other performing animals and prove to have learned the show behaviors without ever being reinforced for them or even doing them. For wild dolphins, apparently, being able to imitate other dolphins must be important for survival.

We can and should use mimicry wherever possible in teaching physical skills to humans—dancing, skiing, tennis, and so on. It's usually wise for the person giving the sample behavior to stand beside or turn his or her back to the subjects, so they can follow the motions with their own bodies without having to do any mental translating. The less deciphering needed, and the less verbal description used, the better the mimicry will work. Incidentally if you want to teach a right-handed skill (crocheting, say) to a left-handed person, you should sit facing him or her and have the subject mimic you, thus executing not the same-sided movements but a mirror image.

Of course a major part of the shaping of the behavior of our children takes place through mimicry. What they see us do, they do too, for better or worse. In my post office one morning recently, three little children were making such a ruckus, it was hard to hear anything else. Their mother, waiting in line, yelled at them several times before she succeeded in frightening them into silence. "How *do* you get kids to be quiet?" she asked the postmistress. "Try speaking softly yourself," the postmistress said, quite correctly. Columnist Judith Martin ("Miss Manners") suggests, when teaching good manners to children, that during the training period—"from birth to marriage"—everybody else in the house will have to eat tidily, speak civilly, and at least feign interest in the doings and conversation of others.

The third shaping shortcut, modeling, consists of pushing the subject manually through the action we want that subject to learn. A golfer does this when he puts his arms around the novice from behind, holds the club, and moves the club and the subject in the desired swing. Some of those who teach sign language to apes employ a lot of modeling. The trainer holds the young chimpanzee's hands and puts them in the desired positions or movements; eventually the ape is supposed to get the picture and make the movements spontaneously. Modeling was the secret of "living statues," a circus act very popular around the turn of the century in which live people and horses were posed to resemble famous paintings or sculptures. The effect that audiences loved was the motionlessness. When the lights went up, there they all were, Napoleon's troops at Waterloo or whatever, caught as if in midmovement—not just the men but the horses, too, with necks arched, forelegs in midair, as if turned to stone. It was done, I am told, by massaging the horses for hours until they were utterly relaxed, and then modeling them like clay into the desired poses and reinforcing them for staying there.

I am always a little dubious about modeling as a training device, even though it is widely used. Until the subject is doing the behavior or at least trying to do the behavior without being held or pushed or modeled, I am not sure much learning takes place. Often all the subject learns is to let you put it through the motions: The dog, being taught to retrieve, learns to let you hold its mouth shut with the dumbbell in its jaws, but when you let go, it lets go; the toddler, put firmly into a high chair, sits quietly while you hold him or her but is up and moving the minute you take your hand away. It's the modeler who gets trained—to hold or guide for longer and longer periods.

It would seem that by putting a subject through the same

motions long enough, or often enough, eventually it would learn how to do the behavior. Sometimes this is true, but eventually can be a long time away, and to go from being pushed through a movement to doing it yourself requires insight: "Aha! They want *me* to do this myself." This is an awful lot to ask of an animal. And even if your subject is an Einstein, repetition in the hope that enlightenment will strike is an inefficient use of valuable training time. The way to make modeling work is to combine it with shaping. While you are putting the subject in position, or through the motions, you stay sensitive to the smallest effort on the subject's part to initiate the proper motion, and that effort is the behavior you reinforce. The dog's jaws tighten on the dumbbell ever so slightly, the golfer begins to swing smoothly, the little chimp's hands move of themselves, and you praise that moment. Then you can shape the new skill while "fading" away the modeling. The combination of modeling and shaping is often an effective way of training behavior; but it is the combination that works and not the modeling alone.

Special Subjects

You can shape behavior in just about any organism. Psychologists have shaped tiny babies to wave their arms to make the lights in the room go off and on. You can shape birds. You can shape fish. I shaped a large hermit crab once to ring a dinner bell by pulling on a string with its claw. (The trick was to get the food to the crab the instant its claw, waving about aimlessly, connected with the string; I used a long pair of dissecting forceps to put bits of shrimp right into the crab's mouthparts.) Harvard professor Richard Herrnstein told me he once shaped a scallop to clap its shell for a food reward. (He didn't tell me how he got the food to the scallop.) Marine mammal trainers like to boast that they can shape *any* animal to do *anything* it is physically and mentally capable of doing, and as far as I can tell, they can.

One of the effects of shaping sessions, especially if they are fruitful experiences for the subject, is to increase attention span; actually you are shaping duration of participation. However, some organisms naturally do not have long attention spans. Immature organisms—puppies, foals, babies—should never be asked for more than three or four repetitions of a given behavior; pressure beyond that may discourage or frighten. This is not to say that immature organisms can't learn. They are learning all the time, but in brief snatches. A fishing captain I know taught his four-month-old granddaughter to "Gimme five!" and the baby's enthusiastic open-handed slap of his palm, in a tiny simulacrum of the jazz musician's greeting, was a never-failing hit with spectators. But he did it in only a few almost momentary "training sessions."

Infancy is not the only biological constraint affecting shaping. Some behaviors come naturally to some species and are difficult for others. Pigs, for example, seem to find it hard to carry something about in their jaws but easy to learn to shove things with their snouts. Most breeds of dogs have been developed for behavioral tendencies as well as looks: One hardly needs to shape a collie to herd sheep, since the necessary stalking behavior has been established, even exaggerated, by breeding; but you'd be giving yourself a tough assignment if you decided to shape sheepherding in a basset hound. Some skills are more easily learned at particular stages of development; a baby mongoose may be tamed and turned into a delightful pet up to the age of six weeks but not after that. Humans are generally thought to acquire languages more easily as children than as adults, although linguists have recently found that an adult who is willing to work at it can probably learn a new language faster than most children and teenagers. One behavior I think is really very difficult to teach to humans in adulthood is swimming. We are among the very few species that do not swim naturally, and while you can teach an adult to float and to make the proper strokes, I have never seen anyone frolic or be at ease in deep water unless he or she learned to swim in childhood.

How about shaping yourself? All kinds of programs exist for changing one's own behavior: SmokeEnders, Weight Watchers, and so on. Most such programs draw heavily on shaping methods, usually called behavior modification, and they may or may not be successful. The difficulty, I think, is that they require you to reinforce yourself. But when you are reinforcing yourself, the event is never a surprise—the subject always knows what the trainer is up to. This makes it awfully easy to say "The heck with getting another star on my chart, I'd rather have a cigarette."

Self-shaping may work for some people. Other people may be successful only after going through three or four different programs, or several repetitions of a given method. Such people can in fact successfully change a habit or give up an addiction, but hardly ever on the first try. Still others may be helped enormously by some form of hypnosis or self-hypnosis. A senior editor at a big publishing house told me that he was able to kick a major cigarette habit by learning, from a hypnotist, to relax into a light trance through self-hypnosis, and to repeat as a mantra or charm a phrase such as "I do not want to smoke" whenever he felt an overpowering urge. For him, as he put it, this technique seemed to "drop a curtain" between him and the cigarette; relief and self-congratulation when the urge had passed was the reinforcer. Whether this is actually what happened or whether other reinforcement contingencies were also in effect is of course impossible to say.

Out of curiosity, while writing this book, I tried out some formal shaping programs, two classroom-taught and two self-administered, for quitting smoking and for learning meditation, weight control, and money management. All were moderately successful but not necessarily at first; some took well over a year. The single most useful device in self-reinforcement, I found, was record keeping, which all four programs made use of. I needed to record performance in such a way that *improvement* could be seen at a glance. I used graphs. Thus my guilt over a lapse could be assuaged by looking at the graphs and seeing that, even so, I was doing much better now than I had been six months previously. Perfection might still be a long way off, but the "curve," or sloping line, of the graph was in the right direction, and this visible proof of improvement, while itself a weak and slow-operating reinforcer, did provide enough motivation to keep me going most of the time.

One kind of self-administered shaping that works beautifully is training by computer. Amusing reinforcements can be built into the computer program so that learning proceeds fast and the shaping experience is fun. It has become an extremely promising application of the laws of positive reinforcement.

Shaping Without Words

In formal training situations, such as a tennis lesson, the subject knows he or she is being shaped and is usually a willing party to the procedure. Thus you don't have to just wait for the response and reinforce it. You can use words to prompt the behavior, and without harm: "Do this. Good. Now do it twice. Good."

In informal situations in real life, however, you are probably better off shaping without instructions or verbal discussion. Suppose you have a messy roommate who leaves dirty clothes all over the place, and verbal instructions—scolding, pleading, whatever— haven't worked. Can you shape neatness? Possibly.

You would of course draw up a shaping plan, the initial and intermediate steps by which you would reach the desired goal. To get dirty clothes into the hamper every time, for example, you might start with one sock, once, and "target" the behavior by holding out the open hamper just as the sock is about to go on the floor. The reinforcer can be verbal, tactile, or whatever you think the roommate would be likely to respond to or accept. People are not dumb; they modify their behavior on just a handful of reinforcers. Even if the scattering of dirty clothes is actually an act of subtle aggression directed against you ("Pick up my clothes, peon!"), by using positive reinforcement you can shape a steady and visible progress toward whatever you consider an adequate level of tidiness.

There are, however, two traps in this use of shaping. The first is that it is easier to notice mistakes than to notice improvement, so, verbal creatures that we are, it is much easier for us to remonstrate when criteria are not met than to reinforce when they are. And that can undo the progress. The second trap is that if you are calculating to shape someone's behavior, it is very tempting to talk about it. And talking about it can ruin it. If you say, "I am going to reinforce you"—for putting your laundry in the hamper, for not smoking marijuana, for spending less, or whatever—you are bribing or promising, not actually reinforcing; on learning of your plans, the person may rebel, instantly, and escalate misbehavior. To get results, you have to *do* the shaping, not talk about it.

And if you do achieve success in shaping someone else's behavior, you better not brag about it later, either. Some shapers never catch on to this and insist on showing off what "they" did—patronizing at best, and a great way to make a lifelong enemy of the subject. Besides, while you may have helped someone improve a skill or get rid of a bad habit by changing your behavior in order to reinforce appropriately, who actually did all the hard work? The subject. Wise parents never go around talking about what a good job they did raising their kids. For one thing, we all know the job is never over, and for another, the kids deserve the credit—if only for surviving all the training mistakes we made.

Because the shaping of people can or even must be tacit, it smacks to some people of an evil sort of manipulativeness. I think this is a misunderstanding. The reason the shaping needs to be nonverbal is that it is behavior we are working with, not ideas, and not just the subjects' behavior but yours as well.

However: Since you can shape people's behavior without their conscious awareness that you are doing so, and since, outside of the formal agreement to be shaped, as in a tennis lesson, you almost have to shape human behavior on the nonverbal level, then isn't it possible to shape people to do horrible things?

Yes, indeed, especially if you are using, as negative reinforcement, an aversive stimulus so severe as to cause real fear, even terror. Psychologists have discovered in the laboratory a phenomenon called learned helplessness. If an animal is taught to avoid an aversive stimulus, such as an electric shock, by pressing a lever or moving to another part of the cage, and is then placed in a cage where there is absolutely no way it can avoid the shock, it will gradually give up trying. It will become completely malleable and passive, and may even lie there and accept punishment when the way to freedom is once again open. "Brainwashing" is possibly a related phenomenon in people. If a person is subjected to severe deprivation and inescapable fear or pain, and if the aversive stimuli are subsequently used as negative reinforcers—that is, as contingencies that the subject can avoid or cause to desist by a change in behavior—well, then . . . animals tend to go to pieces, but people are tougher, and some will do anything they need to do to avoid the negative reinforcement. Let the photographs of Patty Hearst, holding a machine gun in a bank robbery, be evidence. But while her captors did not need a book to tell them how to do that, would we not all be better defended against such events if we understood, each of us, how the laws of shaping work?

3

Stimulus Control: Cooperation Without Coercion

Stimuli

Anything that causes some kind of behavioral response is called a stimulus. Some stimuli can cause responses without any learning or training: We flinch at a loud noise, blink at a bright light, and tend to wander into the kitchen when appetizing smells waft out to us; animals would do the same. Such sounds, lights, and scents are called unconditioned, or primary, stimuli.

Other stimuli are learned by association with a reinforced behavior. They may be meaningless in themselves, but they have become recognizable signals for behavior: Traffic lights make us stop and go, we leap to answer a ringing telephone, on a noisy street we turn at the sound of our own name, and so on and on. In any given day we respond to a multitude of learned signals. These are called stimuli, cues, or signals.

We learn the cues or signals because the behavior we associate with them is one that has a history of being reinforced. Picking up a ringing telephone silences the bell (a negative reinforcer) and brings us a human voice (a positive reinforcer, or so one hopes). The signal or discriminative stimulus sets the stage, or gives us the go-ahead, for a behavior that has in the past led to reinforcement. Conversely, the absence of the stimulus informs us that no reinforcer will be forthcoming for that particular behavior. Pick up a telephone that is not ringing, and all you get is a dial tone.

An enormous part of most formal training efforts consists of establishing discriminative stimuli. The drill sergeant with a platoon of recruits and the dog owner in a training class are equally and primarily concerned with getting trainees to obey commands, which are actually discriminative stimuli. It's not impressive that a dog can sit or a man can halt; what is impressive is that it is done with precision and on command. That is what we call obedience—not merely the acquisition of behaviors but the guarantee that they will be executed when the signal is given. Psychologists call this "bringing behavior under stimulus control." It is hard to train, the training follows rules, and the rules are worth examination.

What if you don't care to boss some dog around and never in your life plan to train a drill team? You can still make use of an understanding of stimulus control. For example, if your kids dawdle and don't come when you call, you have poor stimulus control. If you supervise people, and you sometimes have to give an order or instruction two or three times before it gets done, you have a stimulus-control problem. Did you ever hear these words come out of your mouth: "If I've told you once, I've told you a thousand times, don't . . ." (slam the door, or leave your wet bathing suit on the couch, or whatever)? When telling once *or* a thousand times isn't working, the behavior is not under stimulus control.

We may think we have stimulus control when actually we don't. We expect a signal or command to be obeyed in such cases, and it isn't. One common human reaction is to escalate the signal. The waiter doesn't understand your French? Speak louder. Usually this doesn't work. The subject has to recognize the signal; otherwise it doesn't matter if you yell, or blare it through a rock-band amplification system, you'll still get a blank stare. Another human reaction to failure to get a response to a conditioned stimulus is to get mad. This works only if the subject is exhibiting undesirable behavior or not giving a well-learned response to a well-learned cue. Then sometimes an aversive, such as a time out or a show of temper, can elicit good behavior.

Sometimes the subject responds correctly but after a delay or in a dilatory manner. Often a sluggish response to commands is due to the fact that the subject has not been taught to respond quickly. Without positive reinforcement, not only for the correct response to a cue but also for prompt response, the subject has had no chance to learn that there are benefits in quick obedience to signals. The behavior really isn't under stimulus control.

Real life abounds in bad management of stimulus control. Whenever one person is trying to exert authority, another person is likely to be getting into trouble for "disobedience"; but the real problem is commands that are not understood or signals that can't be obeyed—poor communication or sloppy stimulus control.

Establishing a Cue

Conventional trainers *start* with the cue, before they begin training: "Sit!" Then they push the dog into a sit. After many repetitions, the dog learns to sit, in order to avoid being pushed around, and in due course learns that the word *sit* is his chance to avoid being yanked by exhibiting the sit behavior. Conventional cues or commands are, in fact, conditioned negative reinforcers.

In operant conditioning, on the other hand, we shape the behavior first. Why, after all, would you want to tell the dog to do something it can't possibly understand yet? Once the behavior is secure, we shape the offering of the behavior during or right after some particular stimulus. For example, with the clicker and reinforcers, we develop the behavior of sitting—quickly, neatly, long and often, here on the grass and there on the rug, meeting many criteria—until the dog is offering us sits with great confidence, in the hope of earning reinforcers. Now we introduce the cue as a sort of green light, a chance to earn reinforcers, for that particular behavior. This kind of cue thus becomes a conditioned positive reinforcer: it is guaranteed to lead to reinforcement.

There are several ways to introduce the cue. You may produce the cue just as the behavior is starting, reinforce the completion of the behavior, and then repeat this sequence, at different times and in different locations, gradually backing up the cue in time, until the cue comes before the behavior starts. By and by the learner will identify the cue as the opportunity for that particular behavior to be reinforced: and when you say "Sit," the dog will sit.

A second method—and this is what we used with dolphins— is to alternate between cue and no cue. The behavior is happening frequently. You say "Sit" and click the next sit. Then you let a sit or two go by unclicked and unreinforced. Then you say "Sit" again, and reinforce the sit that follows the cue. You are, in the same training session, reinforcing on-cue sits and extinguishing off-cue sits.

Once your learner understands the rules, new cues can be attached to new behaviors practically instantly this way. However, difficulties may arise with "green" or inexperienced animals learning their first cues. The source of difficulty is the process called *extinction*. Extinction refers to removing a reinforcer for a behavior that used to pay off. It is an aversive experience (Chapter 4) and may engender emotions. I have been soaked from head to foot by a dolphin irate over being unpaid for a behavior that had previously earned a fish.

A third way to add a cue is to shape *response to the cue* as if it were behavior in itself. If this is a puppy's first clicker-trained behavior, you may find the puppy running in front of you and practically tripping you up to show you sits: "Look, I'm doing it, see?" The clicker trainers would say that the dog is "throwing sits at you." This is the perfect time to introduce a cue. The dog is ready to learn a cue, and you need to be able to tell the dog when sitting will work, so it doesn't volunteer the behavior right under your feet when you have your arms full of groceries.

Get out the clicker and treats, say "Sit," and click the first tiny movement of rump toward ground: not the whole behavior, just the start of the movement. Toss the food so the dog has to get on its feet to eat, again say, "Sit" and again click the sit before it's complete. You can make the cue very broad: add a hand signal, body English, speak very clearly. Be sure to cease all those auxiliary cues the instant you click.

Often, in this fashion, one can get a vigorous on-cue sit in just a few clicks. You then return to clicking the sit after the cue but when the rump is fully on the ground (so the dog doesn't start making a habit of half-sits). The next step is to intersperse some other well-learned behavior—perhaps calling the pup over to be patted—between bouts of giving and reinforcing the new sit cue. The last step is to shape the behavior of waiting for the cue—half a second, then a second, then three seconds—until the dog is visibly attending to you and not offering behavior until the cue comes. When that's done, you can start fading out all those auxiliary cues and just using the word. You have developed cue response as an operant behavior, intentionally offered in the hope of gaining reinforcers.

In my observation this is the fastest way to establish both individual cues and the generalization that cues are indicators of which behavior to perform. A woman brought a four-month-old black Labrador puppy, just adopted from a kennel, to one of my seminars. On Saturday at the lunch break I helped her shape the puppy's first clicker-trained behavior, lying down. I feel I am safe in saying that this puppy was clueless, innocent of any training whatsoever. It took a long time just to get the puppy to notice that what it was doing had some effect on the arrival of treats.

That afternoon everyone practiced shaping cue recognition. The next day, at the lunch break, the same owner and same puppy came to my side. Guess what this pup had learned, in twenty-four hours: sit, down, roll over, come, a super "high five" in which the little puppy rolled its weight to the left and threw its right paw straight up as far as it could reach into the air—and the beginnings of a retrieve. All on cue, rapid-fire, correct, and in any order. The puppy, furthermore, was electrified, a totally different dog, attentive, full of fun, muscles all engaged—ready for life.

The Rules of Stimulus Control

There are four aspects to stimulus control. When a dog, by whatever method, has learned to sit when you say "Sit," the job is finished, right?

Wrong. Only half the job is finished. The animal must also be trained—and it is a separate training task—not to sit when it has not been given the command. Bringing behavior under stimulus control is not accomplished until the behavior is also extinguished in the absence of the conditioned stimulus.

This does not mean, of course, that the dog must stand up all day unless you say "Sit." The subject can do what it pleases on its own time. It is in the training or working situation, where discriminative stimuli, or cues and signals, are going to be used, that both the "go" and the "no-go" aspects of a signal must be established if performance is to be reliable.

Complete, perfect stimulus control is defined by four conditions, each one of which may have to be approached as a separate training task, a separate item in the shaping recipe:

1. The behavior always occurs immediately upon presentation of the conditioned stimulus (the dog sits when told to).
2. The behavior never occurs in the absence of the stimulus (during a training or work session the dog never sits spontaneously).
3. The behavior never occurs in response to some other stimulus (if you say "Lie down," the dog does not offer the sit instead).

4. No other behavior occurs in response to this stimulus (when you say "Sit," the dog does not respond by lying down or by leaping up and licking your face).

Only when all four conditions are met does the dog really, fully, and finally understand the command "Sit!" Now you have real stimulus control.

Where, in real life, do we use or need such complete stimulus control? In music, for one example. Orchestra conductors often make very complex use of stimulus control, and, in turn, a conductor in rehearsal may come upon every possible kind of response error. He may, for example, signal for a response—"Forte," more volume, say—and not get it, perhaps because he has not yet clearly established the meaning of the signal. Or he may avoid signaling for more volume and get too much sound anyway. The brass section of classical orchestras is famous for this; Richard Strauss, in a satiric list of rules for young conductors, said, "Never look encouragingly at the brass players." The conductor may signal for another behavior—"Presto," perhaps—and instead of getting faster music, the conductor gets more volume. Tenor soloists seem to do this a lot. Finally, the conductor may ask for more volume and instead get a lot of mistakes. Amateur choruses do this. Each kind of error in response to the cue must be corrected, by training, before the conductor will be satisfied that he or she has adequate stimulus control.

Stimulus control is also vital in the military. The training of rookies in close-order drill, a laborious and time-consuming business, may seem both difficult and meaningless to the recruits, but it has an important function. Not only does it establish prompt response to marching commands, which enables the leaders to move large groups of men about efficiently, but it also trains the skill of responding to learned stimuli in general: obedience to commands, which is after all not just a state of mind but a learned ability, constituting a crucial and often lifesaving skill to a soldier. Ever since armies were invented, close-order drill has been a way of training this skill.

What Kind of Signal?

A discriminative stimulus—a learned signal—can be anything, absolutely anything, that the subject is capable of perceiving. Flags, lights, words, touch, vibration, popping champagne corks— it simply doesn't matter what kind of signal you use. As long as the subject can sense it, the signal can be used to cause learned behavior to occur.

Dolphins are usually trained with visual hand signals, but I know of a blind dolphin that learned to offer many behaviors in response to being touched in various ways. Sheepdogs are usually trained with hand signals and voice commands. In New Zealand, however, where the countryside is wide and the dog may be far off, the signals are often piercing whistles, which carry farther than voice commands. When a shepherd in New Zealand sells such a dog, the buyer may live many miles away; with no way to write down whistles, the old owner teaches the new owner the commands over the telephone or gives him a tape cassette.

Fish will learn to respond to sounds or lights—we all know how fish in an aquarium rush to the top when you tap the glass or turn on the light. And human beings can learn to respond to practically anything.

It is useful, in a working situation, to teach all subjects the same cues and signals, so that other people can cue the same behaviors. Thus animal trainers tend to be quite traditional about the stimuli they use. All over the world horses go forward when you kick their ribs and halt when you pull on the reins. The camels at the Bronx Zoo lie down when they're told "Couche," pronounced "Coosh," even though no one around them, including their trainer, speaks North African French; everybody just knows that's how you're supposed to tell a camel to lie down. That New York camels could just as well learn to lie down on hearing "Cool it, baby" doesn't matter.

Traditional trainers often fail to realize that their signals are mere conventions. Once at a boarding stables I was working with a young horse on a lead line, teaching it "Walk!" as a command. The trainer at the stables looked on with disgust and finally said, "You can't do it that way—horses don't understand 'Walk'; you have to say 'Tch, tch'!" Taking the rope from my hand he said, "Tch, tch," and popped the colt on the rump with the loose rope end, which naturally made the horse start forward. "See?" he said, point proved.

I saw. From then on, wherever I boarded my ponies, I trained them to respond not only to my commands, but to whatever set of giddyaps, gees, haws, and whoas were used by the trainer in charge. It saved trouble, and it made them think I was quite a promising amateur trainer. At least I didn't have my signals crossed!

It was not only possible but easy to train the ponies to two sets of commands. While you don't want more than one behavior occurring on a single stimulus, it's perfectly feasible to have several learned signals for one behavior. For example, in a crowded room a speaker can ask for quiet by shouting "Quiet" or by standing up and raising one hand in a gesture meaning "Hush." Or, if the occupants of the room are noisy, banging a spoon on a water glass will work. We're all conditioned to give this one behavior in response to any of at least three stimuli.

Establishing a second cue for a learned behavior is called transferring the stimulus control. To make a transfer, you present the new stimulus—a voice command, perhaps—first, and then the old one—a hand signal, say—and reinforce the response; then you gradually make the old stimulus less and less obvious while calling attention to the new one by making it very obvious, until the response is given equally well to the new stimulus, even without giving the old one at all. This usually goes quite a bit faster than the training of the original signal; since "Do this behavior" and "Do this behavior on cue" have already been established, "Do this behavior on another cue, too" is more easily learned.

Signal Magnitude and Fading

Learned cues or signals do not have to be of any particular volume or size to get results. A primary, or unconditioned, stimulus produces a gradation of results, depending on its intensity; one reacts more vigorously to a sharp jab than to a pinprick, and the louder the noise, the more it startles. A learned cue, however, merely has to be recognized to lead to the full response. You see a red light and you stop the car; you don't stop faster or slower depending on the size of the light fixture. As long as you recognize the signal you know what to do. Therefore, once a stimulus has been learned, it is possible not only to transfer it but also to make it smaller and smaller, until it is barely perceptible, and still get the same results. Eventually you can get results with a signal so small that it cannot be perceived by a bystander. This is a form of "fading" the stimulus.

We use fading all the time: What has to be a very broad stimulus at first ("No, Dickie, we do not put sand in other children's hair," as you remove Dickie forcibly from the sandbox) becomes, with time, a small signal (merely a lifted eyebrow or wagged index finger). Animal trainers sometimes get wonderful, apparently magical results with faded stimuli. One of the funniest acts I've seen involved a parrot at the San Diego Wild Animal Park that cackled in hysterical laughter in response to a tiny movement of the trainer's hand. You can see the possibilities: "Pedro, what do you think of this man's hat?" "Hahahahaha. . . ." Because the audience did not see the signal, the parrot's single learned behavior seemed the product of a sardonic intelligence cuttingly answering the question; actually, it was a well-timed response to a well-faded stimulus, and the sardonic intelligence, if any, belonged to the trainer, or maybe the scriptwriter.

The best examples of conditioning, fading, and transferring stimuli I have observed occurred not in the world of animal training but in symphony rehearsal halls. As an amateur singer I worked in several opera and symphony choruses, often under guest conductors. While many of the signals conductors give to musicians are more or less standardized, each conductor has personal signals as well. The meaning of these must be established in a very short time; rehearsal time often barely exceeds performance time. Once, in a rehearsal of Mahler's "Resurrection" symphony, just as the basses were about to make their usual booming entrance, I watched the conductor establish an unconditioned stimulus for "Come in softly" by miming an expression of wild alarm and crouching with a hand thrown across his face as if to ward off a blow. Everyone got the message, and in the next few minutes the conductor was able to fade the stimulus, reducing volume in any section of the chorus with a warning glance and a bit of a crouch, or a fleeting echo of the hand gesture, and finally with just a flinch of the shoulder. Conductors also often transfer stimuli by combining a known or obvious gesture—an upward movement of the palm for "Louder," say—with an unknown gesture such as a personal tilt of the head or turn of the body. Sitting on the conductor's left in the alto section, I once saw a guest conductor momentarily transfer all the altos' louder-softer signals to his left elbow.

One result of establishing stimulus control is that the subject must become attentive if it wants to get reinforced for responding correctly, especially if the stimuli are faded. In fact the subject may eventually be able to perceive signals so subtle that the trainer is not even aware of giving them. One classic example is the case of Clever Hans, a horse in Germany at the turn of the century, which was said to be a genius. By pawing with its foot it could count, do arithmetic, spell out words, and even do square roots; right answers were, of course, rewarded with a tidbit. The owner, a retired schoolteacher, truly thought he had taught the horse to read, think, do math, and communicate. Indeed the animal would "answer" questions when the owner was not present.

Many learned gentlemen traveled to Berlin to study Clever Hans and were convinced the horse was a genius. One psychologist, however, eventually demonstrated that the horse was being cued somehow, in that if no one in the room knew the answer, the horse would paw indefinitely. It took much further investigation—over the protests of those who were convinced the horse really was a genius—to demonstrate that the cue to stop pawing was a minuscule lift of the owner's *or any questioner's* head when the right number was reached, a movement originally exaggerated by a broad-brimmed hat the schoolteacher wore but by now so small that it was not only almost impossible to see (except by Clever Hans) but almost impossible to suppress by conscious effort. That was how the horse could tell when to stop pawing from watching people other than its owner.

The Clever Hans phenomenon has now become the name for any circumstance in which apparently amazing behavior, ranging from animal intelligence to psychic phenomena, is actually unconsciously cued by some often-minute or faded behavior of the experimenter that has become a discriminative stimulus for the subject's behavior.

Targeting

A physical target can be a very useful type of discriminative stimulus for all sorts of learners and behaviors. Targeting is a favorite device of many marine mammal trainers; you'll see targets in use at almost any marine park. Trainers hold out a fist for the sea lion to touch, and then move the sea lion around the stage by moving the fist. Dolphins are taught to jump straight up to bump a ball hung high above the water. Sometimes two or three trainers, each with a ball or padded target on a pole, are stationed around the pool to provide a series of targets for a whale swimming from point to point.

Teaching an animal to touch the end of a stick with its nose is an excellent beginning exercise for the new reinforcement trainer. You can see and feel the behavior; it's easy to reinforce, and easy to see how to raise criteria in small steps: two inches from the nose, four inches, to the left, right, up, down, and then forward, until the animal (or the bird, or the fish) is following the target stick around. The owner of a dog training school in Holland told me that one morning she clicker-trained her house cat to target on her coffee spoon and thus was able to lead it all around the breakfast table. The experience was so convincing that she immediately converted her entire school to clicker training.

Zoos use targeting, with clicks and treats, to move tigers and polar bears from one cage to another; to get small animals such as pottos and lemurs to hold still for medication or veterinary inspection; and to separate animals. A video by Gary Priest, curator of behavior at the San Diego Zoo, shows three giraffes learning to touch three individual targets, so that they can be shaped to go calmly into a stall and allow their hooves to be trimmed.

Dog owners have taken to the target stick with alacrity. One can use a target stick to teach a rambunctious, out-of-control dog to walk nicely in heel position. No jerking on the leash, no elaborate training, just longer and longer stretches of "Keep your nose just about *here* for a click and a treat." You can stick the target stick in the ground and use it to teach the dog to go away from you on cue, something obedience competitors often find difficult. You can put the dog through obstacles, or into new places, with a target. Police trainers and search-and-rescue dog trainers are using a laser pointer to send dogs into particular areas. Cats, also, will readily learn to chase the little red dot that the laser pointer projects. It's a great way to have fun with and exercise an indoor cat; and it impresses visitors no end if, for example, your cat, trained with the laser, will jump to the top of the refrigerator on cue.

Target-training, established with a marker signal and treats, can be useful with nonverbal humans, too. A special education teacher told me that she saw marine mammal trainers using targets and immediately applied targeting in her work. One day she was assigned to work with an extremely active little boy with developmental deficits. The work required him to sit at a desk; but their usual classroom was busy, so they were sent to work in the gym. Surrounded by big balls and rockers and climbing equipment, the child, of course, ran off to play. She could not physically make him sit at the table, nor did she want to. So she held out her palm and said "Touch." He did. "Good." With "touch" and "good" she was able to lead him to his chair and keep him there long enough to get the work done, with short bouts of romping inserted periodically. (Knowing you can get your learner back, with a cue such as a target, makes one much more willing to use freedom as a reinforcer!) I have also witnessed targets, including the teacher's hand and the laser pointer, being used to help profoundly low-functioning individuals learn to walk to their classrooms, or desks, or other destinations, voluntarily and without physical guidance—a liberating skill for the learner and the teacher both.

Conditioned Aversive Stimuli as the Cue

The one case where magnitude of a discriminative stimulus might seem to make a difference is in the traditional training of domestic animals. Often the cue—a tug on the reins, or on the leash, a nudge in the horse's ribs—is a watered-down version of the original unconditioned stimulus, the harsher pull or jerk or hard kick that provoked an untrained response. So if the gentle stimulus doesn't work, it seems as if you should get a bigger response with a bigger stimulus. Efforts to put this into practice lead to problems, however.

The learned signal and the primary stimulus are two separate kinds of events, and novices tend to be unaware of this. If they don't get a response to, say, a gentle pull, they pull a little harder, then a little harder than that, all quite futilely, as the horse or dog is pulling with equally increasing force in the opposite direction.

Conventional trainers tend to treat the cue and the use of force separately; they give the signal, and if it is not obeyed, they skip any gradations and immediately elicit the behavior with an extremely strong aversive stimulus—enough to "refresh his memory," as one horse trainer puts it. This is the function of the choke chain used in dog training. Properly taught, even a small person using such a collar can give a quick jerk-and-release powerful enough to knock a Great Dane off its feet. With this primary stimulus in reserve, one can quickly develop good response to a very gentle tug. As British trainer Barbara Woodhouse pointed out, it is in the long run far kinder than perpetually tugging and hauling on the poor beast's neck at some intermediate and meaningless level of force. Shaping the same behavior with positive reinforcers is, of course, even kinder, and also more effective in the short and the long run. Modern dog trainers now use positive reinforcers and a marker signal, such as a word or a click, to accomplish all of the traditional dog behaviors that used to be trained by force.

A discriminative stimulus that is a cue for avoiding an aversive event can not only reduce any need for physical control or intervention, it can even suppress behavior in the trainer's absence. My Border terrier, as a young dog, became fond of digging into the wastebaskets and spreading the contents around. I didn't want to punish her, but I also didn't want to constantly empty the wastebaskets.

I filled a spray bottle with water and added a few drops of vanilla extract: a strong but pleasant scent to me. Then I gritted my teeth and sprayed the dog in the face. She was dismayed and ran. I sprayed the wastebaskets with the scented water. She stayed away from the wastebaskets from then on. There was no need for the scent to be distasteful to her; the stimulus was completely neutral in itself. It was the association that was distasteful. I did find that to maintain her behavior, I had to refresh the stimulus by sprinkling a few drops of vanilla in the wastebaskets about every three months. It was never again necessary to spray the dog.

The same principle is at work in the Invisible Fence systems for keeping a dog on your property. A radio wire is strung around the area in which you want to confine the dog. The dog wears a collar with a receiver in it. If the dog gets too near the line, the collar shocks it. However, a few feet before that point, the collar gives a warning buzz. The warning buzzer is a discriminative stimulus for "Don't go any further." If the setup is properly installed, a trained dog can be effectively confined and will never receive an actual shock. I used such a fence when my terrier and I lived in a house in the woods. An actual fence would have been a perpetual invitation to try to dig under it or escape through an open gate; the conditioned warning signal and the Invisible Fence were far more secure.

Limited Holds

A very useful technique for getting a prompt response to a discriminative stimulus is the limited hold. Let us say your subject has learned to offer a behavior in response to a cue, but there is usually some gap in time between presentation of the stimulus and the subject's response. You call folks for supper, and in due course they come; or you signal a halt, and your elephant gradually slows to a stop.

If you wish, by using a limited hold, you can actually shape this interval downward until the behavior occurs as fast as is physically possible. You start by estimating the normal interval in which the behavior usually occurs; then you reinforce only behavior that occurs during that interval. Since living creatures are variable, some responses will fall outside the interval, and those no longer earn reinforcers. For example, if you serve supper a set time after calling, rather than waiting for stragglers, stragglers may get cold food or less choice of food.

When you set a time interval like this and reinforce only within it, you will find that gradually all responses fall within that interval and no more are occurring outside it. Now you can tighten the screws again. Does it take fifteen minutes for the family to gather? Start serving twelve minutes after you call, or ten. How fast you tighten the screws is strictly a matter of judgment; as in any shaping procedure, you want to stay within the range where most of the behavior is occurring most of the time.

Animals and people have a very sharp time sense and will respond to limited-hold training with dramatic precision, but the trainer should not rely on guesswork. Use the clock, even a stopwatch, if you want limited-hold training to happen for you. On briefer behaviors, count to yourself, getting response time down from five beats to two, say. And of course, if you are working in a human situation, don't discuss what you are doing; you'll get nothing but arguments. Just do it and watch it work.

At Sea Life Park in the 1960s one of our most effective show highlights was a group of six little spinner dolphins performing several kinds of aerial acrobatics in unison. They did various leaps and whirls in response to underwater sound cues. Initially, when the cue went on, the leaps or spins, or whatever was called for, occurred raggedly and sporadically across a fifteen- to twenty-second period. By using a stopwatch and establishing a limited hold, we were able to crank down the performance interval to two and a half seconds. Every animal knew that in order to get a fish it had to hit the air and perform the right leap or spin within two and a half seconds of the time the cue went on. As a result, the animals poised themselves attentively near the underwater loudspeaker. When the cue went on, the pool erupted in an explosion of whirling bodies in the air; it was quite spectacular. One day while sitting among the audience, I was amused to overhear a professorial type firmly informing his companions that the only way we could be getting that kind of response was by electric shock.

Limited holds in real life are simply the amount of time you are willing to wait for a request or instruction to be carried out. Parents, bosses, and teachers who are consistent as to what they expect, once the specific time interval has been established, are usually regarded as fair and reliable to deal with, even if the limited hold—the "window" in time during which the behavior must occur in order to be reinforced—is quite brief.

Anticipation

A common flaw in stimulus-controlled behavior is anticipation: Once the cue has been learned, the subject is so eager to offer the behavior that it acts before the cue has actually been given. The expression describing this event comes from human anticipatory behavior in footraces: jumping the gun. People who anticipate cues or requests of others are generally perceived to be overeager, fawning, or obsequious; it's an irritating habit, not a virtue.

Doberman pinschers sometimes run into trouble in obedience competitions. Although they are marvelously trainable dogs, they are so alert that they anticipate commands by the smallest of hints and often work before they have actually been told to, thus losing points. Anticipation is a common fault in calf-roping horses in rodeos. The cowboy and horse are supposed to wait behind a barrier for the calf to be given a head start, but the horse, excited, plunges off before the signal. The cowboy sometimes thinks he's got a real goer, but what he's really got is incompletely trained stimulus control. Another very common occurrence of anticipation is the "offsides" call in football. One player is so eager that he moves into the other team's territory before the signal to play is given, and the team must be penalized.

One way to cure anticipation is to use time-outs. If the subject anticipates the cue, and if that is undesirable, stop all activity. Give no cues and do nothing for one full minute. Every time the subject jumps the gun again, reset the clock. You are penalizing overeagerness by making it the cause of delay of the chance to work. This will effectively extinguish anticipating a command when rebuke, punishment, or repetition might have no effect at all.

Stimuli as Reinforcers: Behavior Chains

Once a conditioned stimulus is established, an interesting thing happens: It becomes a reinforcer. Think of the recess bell in school. The recess bell is a signal meaning "You're excused, go out and play." And yet it is perceived as a reinforcer—children are glad to hear it, and if they could do something to make it ring sooner, they would. Now imagine a recess bell that did not ring unless the classroom was quiet. Around recess time you would get some very quiet classrooms.

A discriminative stimulus signals the opportunity for reinforcement, so it becomes a desirable event. A desirable event is in itself a reinforcer. That means that you can actually reinforce a behavior by presenting the stimulus for another behavior. For example: If I reward my cat with a tidbit for coming to me when I say "Come," and she learns this and does it, and if I then say "Come" and reinforce her for doing so each time I happen to see her sitting on the mantelpiece, it will soon happen that the cat, wanting a tidbit, will be found on the mantelpiece. (From her standpoint, remember, she is training me; she has found a way to get me to say "Come.") Now suppose I teach her to jump to the mantel when I point to it, using either food or "Come" as the reinforcer; and then I point to the mantel whenever (a) I know she is hungry, and (b) she happens to roll on her back . . .

I have trained a behavior chain.

Behavior chains are very common. We often do long series of connected behaviors in real life, behaviors involving many known steps—carpentry and housework come to mind—and we expect our animals to do the same: "Come," "Sit," "Down," "Heel," and so on at length, with no obvious reinforcement. These long strings of behavior are behavior chains. Unlike simple long-duration behaviors—do this for an hour, do this a hundred times—they can be maintained comfortably, without deterioration or delayed starts, because each behavior is actually reinforced by the signal or opportunity to perform the next behavior, until the final reinforcement of a job completed.

There are several kinds of behavior chains. *Homogeneous* chains are chains in which the same behavior is repeated over and over again, like a horse going over a series of identical jumps in a row. *Heterogeneous* chains consist of various different behaviors that are reinforced only when the last behavior is completed. Most formal dog obedience competition exercises are heterogeneous chains. In one midlevel exercise, for example, the dog is required (1) to sit at the owner's side while the owner tosses a dumbbell beyond a jump, and then (2) on hearing the cue, go over the jump and (3) locate and pick up the dumbbell and (4) turn around and jump back over the jump while carrying the dumbbell and (5) sit in front of the owner until the owner takes the dumbbell and (6) return, on cue, to the sit-at-heel position. In competition these chains are always performed in the same sequence. They may, however, be trained as individual behaviors or as parts of the chain in other sequences.

The pattern of the sequence is not essential to the nature of a chain. What is essential is that the behaviors in the chain follow each other without a time gap, that they are governed by cues, either from the trainer or from the environment, and that the primary reinforcer occurs at the end of the chain. The same dog, in a hunting or herding trial, might perform a long series of learned behaviors that might vary considerably in sequence from one day to the next depending on the environment. The whole sequence, however, would eventually be reinforced when the pheasant is retrieved or the sheep are in the pen.

What makes behavior chains work is that each behavior has a history of reinforcement, and each behavior is under stimulus control, or on cue. Thus the learned cues, which are guarantees of future reinforcers, maintain behaviors within the chain. The cues can be given by a handler: The shepherd, with whistles, can tell the sheepdog exactly which way to turn, how fast to go, when to stop, and when to return. The cues can also be provided by the environment. Once the obedience competition dog has gone over the jump, the sight of the dumbbell is the cue to pick it up, the pickup is a cue to return to the owner, and the sight of the jump is the cue to jump back over it again. The owner need not provide verbal cues for those parts of the chain, but the cues are there.

Sometimes the cue for the next behavior consists of the previous behavior. I recently moved to a new city and established both a new residence and a new place of business. I memorized the new addresses, phone numbers, fax numbers, and e-mails, but for many months I could not give you just a part of any one of those chains. Ask me for the office zip code and I was stumped, unless I said the name of the town and state first, then the zip code reeled out. Same thing for phone numbers: I *had* to say the area code to recite the rest of the number—an internally cued behavior chain.

Many things we do every day, such as taking a shower and getting dressed, are behavior chains of this nature. In teaching people with developmental deficits, behavior analysts find that constructing carefully cued and reinforced behavior chains is extremely useful in giving people the skills they need to live independently or semi-independently.

We recognize that behavior chains are useful and powerful. What we don't always recognize, however, is that what we see as misbehavior is often just a result of a chain breaking down. In teaching operant conditioning to dog trainers, I have heard many other explanations for misbehavior—the dog is stubborn; the dog is just trying to get back at me; the dog is stressed/in heat/just out of heat/and so on—when the incorrect events, in fact, are the result of the trainer's failure to build or maintain a behavior chain.

Behavior chains break down and the behavior goes to pieces if there are unlearned behaviors in the chain, or behaviors that have not been brought under stimulus control. You can't reinforce the subject with a cue if it doesn't recognize the cue, or if it cannot accomplish what the cue indicates. This means that behavior chains should be trained *backward*. Start with the last behavior in the chain; make sure it has been learned and that the signal to begin it is recognized; then train the next-to-last one, and so on. For example, in memorizing a poem, a piece of music, a speech, or lines in a play, if you divide the task up into, say, five sections, and memorize the sections in reverse order, starting with the last, you will always be going from weakness to strength, from the stuff you're not quite sure of yet into the great, reinforcing, well-memorized stuff you know cold. Memorizing material in the order in which it is written and will be presented necessitates plowing continuously from familiar ground into the more difficult and unknown, a most *unreinforcing* experience. Treating memorization tasks as behavior chains not only shortens the needed memorizing time considerably, it also makes the whole experience more pleasant.

Behavior chains are a peculiar concept. I've often been thwarted by them myself, feeling that I'm pushing at the end of a string because I can't get an animal, or a child, or myself, to do some apparently simple series of things, until I realize that I'm trying to train a behavior chain from the wrong end. When you make a cake, the frosting goes on last; but if you want to teach a child to enjoy making a cake, you start by asking for "help" with the frosting.

AN EXAMPLE OF A BEHAVIOR CHAIN: TEACHING A DOG TO PLAY FRISBEE

A New York friend who takes his golden retriever to Central Park each weekend to play Frisbee tells me the world seems to be full of people who have been stymied in trying to teach their dog this game. This is a pity, because playing Frisbee is an excellent way to exercise a big dog in the city. The Frisbee is a much slower and more erratic target than a simple ball, more like real prey perhaps, encouraging the dog into leaps and fancy catches that are fun for the owner, too. And playing Frisbee allows the owner to stand in one place and still run the dog's legs off.

What people complain of is that their dog, when encouraged, will leap for the Frisbee and try to grab it as it is waved around, but when they throw it, the dog just stands there and watches it go. Or the dog chases and grabs it, but never brings it back.

There are two training problems in this game: The first is that the distance the dog goes after the Frisbee must be shaped. The second is that the game is a behavior chain: First the dog chases the Frisbee, then the dog catches the Frisbee, then the dog brings the Frisbee back for another throw. So each behavior must be trained separately, and the last behavior in the chain, retrieving, must be trained first.

You can teach retrieving over very short distances—indoors,

even—with something easy to hold: an old sock, maybe. Hunting dogs almost do it spontaneously. Other breeds, such as bulldogs and boxers, may have to be carefully shaped to drop or give back the item, since they tend to prefer playing tug-of-war.

When the dog will carry things to you on cue and give them up, you shape catching the Frisbee. First you get the dog all excited about the Frisbee, waving it around his face. You let him take it and have him give it back a few times, praising him madly for returning it, of course. Then you hold it in the air, let him have it when he leaps for it, and make him give it back. Then you toss it momentarily into the air and make a big fuss when he catches it. When he has the idea, you can start shaping the first behavior of the chain, the chase, by tossing the Frisbee up and out from you a few feet so the dog has to move off after it, to catch it. And now you are on your way to having a great Frisbee dog.

As the distance grows longer, the dog needs to learn to watch the Frisbee and place himself well for the catch. This takes practice, so it might take a couple of weekends to get the dog going out twenty-five feet or so. A fast dog will eventually be able to get under and catch a Frisbee as far as you can throw it—the star Frisbee dog Ashley Whippet could catch a Frisbee thrown the length of a football field. Dogs seem to relish their own expertise. A brilliant run or a terrific over-the-shoulder four-legs-off-the-ground catch that brings cheers from spectators also makes the dog sparkle all over. Nevertheless, after that catch the dog brings the Frisbee back because you trained that end of the chain first, and because that is what earns him the reinforcement, whether it is praise from you or another toss of the Frisbee.

Of course you can see that if you are inattentive, so that he repeatedly gets neither the praise nor the toss, retrieving will deteriorate. Also, when the dog is getting too tired to play anymore, he will begin to falter on the retrieve by coming in slowly or dropping the Frisbee en route. This means it is high time to quit—you've both had your fun.

Generalized Stimulus Control

With most animals, you have to go to some lengths to establish stimulus control at first, but often by the time you start bringing the third or fourth behavior under stimulus control, you will find that the animal seems to have generalized, or come to some conceptual understanding. After learning three or four cued behaviors, most subjects seem to recognize that certain events are signals, each signal means a different behavior, and acquiring reinforcers depends upon recognizing and responding correctly to signals. From then on, establishment of learned stimuli is easy. The subject already has the picture, and all it has to do is learn to identify new signals and associate them with the right behaviors. Since you, as trainer, are helping all you can by making that very clear, subsequent training can itself go much faster than the initial laborious steps.

People generalize even faster. If you reward responses to even one learned command, people rapidly start responding to other commands to earn reinforcement. My friend Lee, a sixth-grade math teacher in one of the rough parts of New York City, always begins the school year by training his pupils to get rid of their chewing gum when he tells them to. No coercion. Just "Okay, everybody, the first thing we're going to do is take our chewing gum out of our mouths. Good! Oops, wait, Doreen's still got some . . . great! She took it out! Let's hear it for Doreen." He also instructs them, at the end of class, to resume chewing gum (using "Class dismissed" as the reinforcer). This might seem frivolous, even silly (though it does spare Lee the sight of masticating jaws, which he hates), but he finds that this first exercise awakens his class to the possibility of earning reinforcement by responding to his requests.

Of course, like a good killer whale trainer, he uses a variety of reinforcers besides good grades and his own approval, including games, peer approval, early dismissal, even free gum. And of course at first he is willing to spend considerable time on gum that might be spent on fractions; his kids think he is weird about gum. But his kids also learn he means what he says, and that it pays off to do what he wants; so they become generally responsive and attentive.

The other teachers think Lee has some inborn knack for keeping his classroom quiet, and the principal thinks he's a "good disciplinarian." Lee thinks kids are bright enough to generalize their responses, and he loves them for doing so. And for not chewing gum.

Prelearning Dips and Tantrums

Bringing behavior under stimulus control often gives rise to an interesting phenomenon I call the "prelearning dip." You have shaped a behavior, and now you are bringing it under stimulus control. But just as the subject seems to be showing signs of responding to the stimulus, it suddenly not only stops responding to the stimulus, it stops responding altogether. It acts as if it has never heard of the thing you have shaped it to do.

This can be most discouraging for the trainer. Here you have cleverly taught a chicken to dance, and now you want it to dance only when you raise your right hand. The chicken looks at your hand, but it doesn't dance. Or it may stand still when you give the signal and then dance furiously when the signal is not present.

If you were to graph this sequence, you would see a gradually climbing line as the subject's percentage of correct responses (that is, on-cue responses) increases, followed by a sharp dip as correctness falls to zero (as you get a bunch of nonresponses or wrong responses). After that, however, if you persist, illumination strikes: Suddenly, from total failure, the subject leaps to responding very well indeed—you raise your hand, the chicken dances. The behavior is under stimulus control.

What is going on, in my opinion, is that at first the subject is learning the cue without really being aware of doing so; the trainer sees only a heartening tendency toward slowly increasing correct performance. But then the subject *notices* the cue, and becomes aware that the signal has something to do with whether it gets reinforced. At that point it attends to the signal rather than offering the behavior. Of course it gives no response and goes unreinforced. When, by coincidence or the trainer's perseverance, it does once again offer the behavior in the presence of the cue, and it does get reinforced, the subject "gets the picture." From then on, it "knows" what the cue means and responds correctly and with confidence.

I realize I am throwing a lot of words around here, such as "aware" and "knows," referring to what is going on in the subject's head, which most psychologists do not like to see applied to animals. Also, it's true that sometimes, in training an animal, the level of correct response gradually increases without any big events occurring; it would be hard to say at what point, if ever, the animal becomes consciously aware of what it is doing. But when a prelearning dip does occur, I think it is a sign of a shift in awareness, no matter what species is involved. I have seen in the data of University of Hawaii researcher Michael Walker clear-cut prelearning dips (and consequently some kind of awareness shift) during sensory-discrimination experiments with tuna, one of the more intelligent sorts of fishes, but after all, merely a fish.

For the subject, the prelearning dip can be a very frustrating time. We all know how upsetting it is to struggle with something we half-understand (math concepts are a common example), knowing only that we don't really understand it. Often the subject feels so frustrated that it exhibits anger and aggression. The child bursts into tears and stabs the math book with a pencil. Dolphins breach repeatedly, slapping their bodies against the surface of the water with a crash. Horses switch their tails and want to kick. Dogs growl. Dr. Walker found that if, during the training of stimulus recognition, he let his tuna make mistakes and go unreinforced for more than forty-five seconds at a time, they got so upset, they jumped out of the tank.

I have come to call this the "prelearning temper tantrum." It seems to me that the subject has the tantrum because what it has always thought to be true turns out suddenly not to be true; and there's no clear reason why . . . yet. In humans prelearning temper tantrums often seem to take place when long-held beliefs are challenged and the subject *knows* deep inside that there is some truth to the new information. The recognition that what has been learned is not quite true seems to lead to the furious comeback, to excessive response, far beyond the disagreement, discussion, or querying that might offhand seem more probable and appropriate. Sometimes when talking about reinforcement at scientific meetings, I have provoked more hostility than I expected from individuals in other disciplines, ranging from cognitive psychologists to neurologists to an Episcopal bishop. I often suspect the angry words are actually prelearning symptoms.

I am always sorry to see the prelearning temper tantrum occur, even in a tuna, because with skill one should be able to lead the subject through the learning transition without arousing so much frustration. However, I have come to regard the prelearning tantrum as a strong indicator that real learning is actually finally about to take place. If you stand back and let it pass over, like a rainstorm, there may be rainbows on the other side.

The Uses of Stimulus Control

Nobody needs to control or be controlled by cues and signals all the time; living creatures are not a bunch of machines. Most of the time there's no need to boss the world around. If the kids dawdle and you're not in a hurry, you can slow down yourself. Employees who are already working hard don't need orders and instructions. There's no point in surrounding ourselves or others with unnecessary rules and regulations; that only breeds resistance. In fact, responding to learned signals is an effort, and an effort that not only shouldn't be but can't be carried on continuously.

Stimulus control is obviously involved in producing cooperative children, obedient pets, reliable staff members, and so on. Very specific stimulus control is also necessary for many group activities, such as marching bands, dance troupes, and team sports. There is a certain amount of satisfaction in responding to elaborate sets of learned signals; even animals seem to enjoy it. I think this is because the signals become reinforcers, as in a behavior chain, so that once one has mastered all behaviors and signals, executing the responses brings a lot of reinforcement. In a word, it is fun. Hence the fun of participating in signal-controlled group activities, such as square dancing, playing football, and singing or playing music in groups.

When we see some example of beautifully executed stimulus-controlled behavior—from the navy's acrobatic jet-plane team, the Blue Angels, to a classroom of well-mannered children—we often praise it in terms of discipline: "They are really well disciplined" or "That teacher knows how to maintain discipline." The word *discipline,* however, contains implications of punishment, which, as we've seen, is quite unnecessary in the establishment of stimulus control.

In popular parlance the disciplinarian is the coach, parent, or trainer who demands perfection and punishes anything less, not the one who approaches perfection by rewarding improvement in that direction. And so it is that people who set out to establish "discipline" often tend to try to get stimulus control on a "Do what I say or *else* . . ." basis. Since the subject has to misbehave or disobey to find out what the "or *else*" is, and since by then it's too late to undo the behavior, this ever-popular approach doesn't work very well.

Real, elegant stimulus control, established through use of shaping and reinforcers, may produce something we interpret as discipline in the subject. The person who really has to become disciplined, however, is the trainer.

Yes, *but* where do you begin? What if you live or work among people who are already confirmed signal ignorers? Here is the Karen Pryor system of effecting a change in a hard case:

Karen Pryor   (Seeing a young visitor's wet bathing suit and towel on the living-room couch): Please take your wet things off the couch and put them in the dryer.

Young Visitor: Okay, in a minute.

K.P. (Physically goes to the young visitor and stands there, saying nothing.)

Y.V.:   What's the matter with you?

K.P.:   Please take your wet bathing suit off the couch and put it in the dryer. (N.B: Without adding "Now!" or "Right this minute," or "I mean it," or anything else. I am training this person to obey requests the first time, not to wait until the signal has been heightened with further details or threats.)

Y.V.:   Well, jeez, if you're in such a hurry, why don't you do it yourself?

K.P. (Pleasant smile, no comment. I am waiting to reinforce the behavior I want. Giving me an argument is not the behavior I want, so I ignore it.)

Y.V.:   Okay, okay. (Gets up, goes to couch, picks up stuff, tosses it at the laundry room.)

K.P.:   In the dryer.

Y.V. (Grumbling, puts stuff in the dryer.)

K.P. (Big smile, sincere, no sarcasm): *Thank* you!

The next time I have to ask the young visitor to do something, probably all I'll have to do is look at him to get action. By and by he will be one of the people in the household who do what I ask promptly, and for my part I will be fair—I'll do what *he* asks, if it's feasible, and I'll be careful not to ask him to do more than his share.

Knowing how to get stimulus control without resorting to uproar and coercion makes life a lot easier for everyone, trainer and subject alike. When my daughter, Gale, was a junior in high school, she directed a class play—something a student was chosen to do every year. She had a big cast of about twenty boys and girls. Everything went well, and the play was a great success. At the closing performance the drama coach told me that she'd been amazed to see that throughout rehearsals Gale never yelled at her cast. Student directors always yell, but Gale never yelled. "Of course not," I said without thinking, "she's an animal trainer." From the look on the teacher's face, I realized I'd said the wrong thing—her students were not animals! But of course all I meant was that Gale would know how to establish stimulus control without unnecessary escalation.

People who have a disciplined understanding of stimulus control avoid giving needless instructions, unreasonable or incomprehensible commands, or orders that can't be obeyed. They try not to make requests they're not prepared to follow through on; you always know exactly what they expect. They don't fly off the handle at a poor response. They don't nag, scold, whine, coerce, beg, or threaten to get their way, because they don't need to. And when you ask *them* to do something, if they say yes, they do it. When you get a whole family, or household, or corporation working on the basis of real stimulus control—when all the people keep their agreements, say what they need, and do what they say—it is perfectly amazing how much gets done, how few orders ever need to be given, and how fast the trust builds up. Good stimulus control is nothing more than true communication— honest, fair communication. It is the most complex, difficult, and elegant aspect of training with positive reinforcement.

4

Untraining:
Using Reinforcement
to Get Rid of Behavior
You Don't Want

Now that you know all about establishing new behavior, how do you get rid of behavior you don't want that's already happening?

People and animals are always doing things we wish they wouldn't do. The kids scream and fight in the car. The dog barks all night. Cats claw the furniture. Your roommate leaves dirty laundry all over the place. A relative repeatedly makes quarrelsome, demanding phone calls. These are unwanted behaviors.

There are eight methods of getting rid of a behavior. Only eight. It doesn't matter if it's a long-term behavior such as the messy roommate or a short-term problem such as kids making too much noise in the car; anything you do about it is going to be a variation of one of the eight methods. (I am not concerned with complex constellations of behavioral problems such as arise in the psychotic person or the unpredictably dangerous dog; I am considering only single items of undesirable behavior.)

The eight methods are:

- **Method 1**: "Shoot the animal." (This definitely works. You will never have to deal with that particular behavior in that particular subject again.)
- **Method 2**: Punishment. (Everybody's favorite, in spite of the fact that it almost never really works.)
- **Method 3**: Negative reinforcement. (Removing something unpleasant when a desired behavior occurs.)
- **Method 4**: Extinction; letting the behavior go away by itself.
- **Method 5**: Train an incompatible behavior. (This method is especially useful for athletes and pet owners.)
- **Method 6**: Put the behavior on cue. (Then you never give the cue. This is the dolphin trainer's most elegant method of getting rid of unwanted behavior.)
- **Method 7**: "Shape the absence"; reinforce anything and everything that is *not* the undesired behavior. (A kindly way to turn disagreeable relatives into agreeable relatives.)
- **Method 8**: Change the motivation. (This is the fundamental and most kindly method of all.)

You can see that there are four "bad fairies," or negative methods, and four "good fairies," or methods using positive reinforcement. Each has its place. I'm going to describe the pros and cons of each method, one by one, together with some anecdotes of circumstances in which that method has worked. I'm also going to include under each method a repeated set of familiar problems (the noisy dog, the crabby spouse, and so on) with examples of how each problem could be solved by each particular method.

I don't recommend all these solutions. For example, I think

having a veterinarian "debark" your dog by cutting its vocal cords (Method 1) is a lousy solution to the problem of a dog that barks all night. I say that even though my uncle John Slater resorted to this solution, with my reluctant approval, when the neighbors complained about the barking of his sea lions. Of course, not many people keep sea lions in their swimming pool. Maybe it's the method of choice in that case.

I cannot tell you which of the eight methods is the method of choice for getting rid of your particular nuisance. You're the trainer; you have to decide.

Method 1: "Shoot the Animal"

This always works. You will definitely never have that behavioral problem with that subject again. This is in fact the worldwide and only recognized method of dealing with dogs that take to killing sheep.

Capital punishment is Method 1. Whatever the moral and other implications of capital punishment may be, if you execute a murderer, he certainly will not be able to do any more murdering. Method 1 gets rid of the behavior by getting rid of the doer, temporarily or permanently.

Firing an employee, divorcing a spouse, dealing with a messy roommate by changing roommates: all are Method 1. New problems with new people may come along, but the subject whose behavior you are specifically fed up with is gone, and the behavior goes away, too.

Method 1 is pretty severe, but it is sometimes appropriate when the offense is too major to endure and seems unlikely to be easily modified. For example, suppose your parent or your spouse (or your child) beats you. People sometimes deal with this by actually eliminating the person, and in extreme cases of self-defense this could be justifiable. Leaving home is another Method 1 solution, and more humane.

I once had a cat that developed the peculiar habit of stealing into the kitchen in the night and urinating on the stove burners. The odor, when you unknowingly turned on one of those burners the next day, was incredibly offensive. The cat had free access to the outdoors, I never caught her at the behavior, and if you covered the burners she urinated on the covers. I could not decipher her motivation, and I finally took that cat to the pound to be put to sleep. Method 1.

There are many simple and common versions of Method 1: sending a child to his or her room for disturbing adult conversation; tying up the dog so it can't chase cars; putting people in prison for varying lengths of time. We tend to think of these things as punishment (Method 2), and they may or may not be seen as punishments by the subjects, but these are Method 1 techniques. Fundamentally they eliminate the behavior by restraining the subject physically from the performance, or by eliminating the presence of the subject.

The vital thing to understand about Method 1 is that it teaches the subject nothing. Preventing the subject from exhibiting the behavior—by restraint, confinement, divorce, electrocution— does not teach the subject much about the behavior. It seems reasonable that a man sent to prison for theft will think twice before he steals again, but we know that very often that is far from the case; all we can be sure of is that he cannot rip off your TV while he is locked up.

Behavior is not necessarily reasonable. If it has already been established as a way to earn reinforcement, and if the motivation and circumstances that elicit the behavior are present, the behavior is likely to manifest itself again.

While the subject is under restraint, no relearning about the behavior goes on; you cannot modify behavior that is not occurring. The child shut up in his or her room may be learning something (to resent and fear you, perhaps) but not how to engage in polite social conversation. Let that dog off the rope, and it will promptly chase cars again.

Method 1 has its place. It is often the most practical solution, and it is not necessarily cruel. We often use some kind of temporary

SAMPLES OF METHOD 1:
"SHOOT THE ANIMAL"

Method 1 solves the problem in a way but may or may not be the method of choice in any given situation.

BEHAVIOR	APPROACH
Roommate leaves dirty laundry all over the place.	Change roommates.
Dog in yard barks all night.	Shoot the animal. Sell it. Have its vocal cords cut by the vet.
Kids too noisy in the car.	Make them walk home. Make them take the bus. Get someone else to drive the car pool.
Spouse habitually comes home in a bad mood.	Divorce.
Faulty tennis swing.	Stop playing tennis.
Shirking or lazy employee.	Fire him or her.
Hating to write thank-you notes.	Never write any thank-you notes. Then maybe people will stop giving you presents.
Cat gets on the kitchen table.	Keep the cat outdoors or get rid of it.
Surly bus driver is rude to you and makes you mad.	Get off the bus and take the next one.
An adult offspring who you think should be self-sufficient wants to move back in with you.	Say no and stick to it.

incarceration when we don't have time to train or supervise a subject. We put babies in swings or baby seats to amuse themselves briefly, and for short periods most babies have no objections. Now that most people keep their pet dogs indoors all the time, confining puppies to shipping boxes called crates has become a standard aid to housebreaking. Dogs like having a cozy, private place to sleep in. Most dogs quickly regard their crate as home and will retire to it voluntarily during the day.

Even small puppies prefer not to soil their sleeping quarters. So confinement when you can't watch the puppy reduces the chance of accidents and usually means that the puppy is ready for an educational and reinforced trip to the yard to relieve itself, when you do take it out. For long confinements the puppy is commonly put in a wire exercise pen with newspaper on the floor and the crate, door ajar, in one corner. Thus it has room to romp around and play, it can leave the crate if it needs to piddle, it's easily cleaned up after, and at least it's not making spots on the rug in the owner's absence.

Method 2: Punishment

This is humanity's favorite method. When behavior goes wrong, we think first of punishment. Scold the child, spank the dog, dock the paycheck, fine the company, torture the dissident, invade the country. But punishment is a clumsy way of modifying behavior. In fact, much of the time punishment doesn't work at all.

Before considering what punishment can and cannot do, let us note what happens when we try it and it doesn't work. Suppose we have punished a child, or a dog, or an employee for some behavior, and the behavior occurs again. Do we say, "Hmm, punishment isn't working; let's try something else"? No. We escalate the punishment. If scolding doesn't work, try a slap. If your kid has a bad report card, take away his bike. If the next report card is also bad, take away his skateboard, too. Your employees are

SAMPLES OF METHOD 2: PUNISHMENT

These are seldom effective and lose effect with repetition but are widely used.

BEHAVIOR	APPROACH
Roommate leaves dirty laundry all over the place.	Yell and scold. Threaten to confiscate and throw away the clothes, or do so.
Dog in yard barks all night.	Go out and hit him or spray him with the hose when he barks. (N.B.: Dog will be so glad to see you, he'll probably "forgive" the punishment.)
Kids too noisy in the car.	Yell at them. Threaten. Turn around and smack them.
Spouse habitually comes home in a bad mood.	Start a fight. Burn the dinner. Sulk, scold, cry.
Faulty tennis swing.	Curse, get mad, criticize yourself every time you do it wrong.
Shirking or lazy employee.	Scold and criticize, preferably in front of others. Threaten to dock pay, or do so.
Hating to write thank-you notes.	Punish yourself by postponing the task and feeling guilty at the same time.
Cat gets on the kitchen table.	Strike it and/or chase it out of the kitchen.
Surly bus driver is rude to you and makes you mad.	Obtain the driver's number, complain to the company, and try to get him or her transferred, reprimanded, or fired.
An adult offspring who you think should be self-sufficient wants to move back in with you.	Let the adult child move in but make life miserable for him or her.

goofing off? Threaten them. Doesn't work? Dock their pay. Still no results? Suspend them, fire them, call out the National Guard. Whippings do not change the heretic's behavior? Maybe thumbscrews will work, or the rack.

The hideous thing about the escalation of punishment is that there is absolutely no end to it. The search for a punishment so bad that "maybe *this* one will work" is not a concern of apes or elephants, but it has preoccupied humans since history began and probably before.

One reason punishment doesn't usually work is that it does not coincide with the undesirable behavior; it occurs afterward, and sometimes, as in courts of law, long afterward. The subject therefore may not connect the punishment to his or her previous deeds; animals never do, and people often fail to. If a finger fell off every time someone stole something, or if cars burst into flames when they were parked illegally, I expect stolen property and parking tickets would be nearly nonexistent.

In Method 2, as in Method 1, the subject learns nothing. While prompt punishment may *stop* an ongoing behavior, it does not cause any particular improvement to occur. Punishment does not teach a child how to achieve a better report card. The most the punisher can hope for is that the child's motivation will change: The child will try to alter future behavior in order to avoid future punishment.

Learning to alter behavior in the future in order to avoid consequences in the future is more than most animals can understand. If a man catches his bird dog and beats it because it has been chasing rabbits, the dog has no way of knowing which particular recent activity is being reprimanded. It may become more fearful of the owner, which might allow the owner, from then on, to call it off when it chases rabbits, or might cause the dog to run away even faster when called. The beating in itself will not affect rabbit chasing in itself.

Cats, incidentally, seem particularly dense about associating their punishments with their crimes. Like birds, they merely become frightened when threatened, and they learn nothing, which is why people think cats are difficult to train. They really can't be trained by punitive methods, but they're a snap to train with positive reinforcement.

While punishment or the threat of it doesn't help the subject learn how to modify the behavior involved, what the subject does learn—especially if the behavior is so strongly motivated that the subject *needs* to continue it (stealing food when hungry, being one of the gang during adolescence)—is to try not to get caught. Evasiveness increases rapidly under a punishment regimen—a sad situation in a family setting and not so great in society at large either. Also, repeated or severe punishment has some very nasty side effects: fear, anger, resentment, resistance, even hate in the punished one and sometimes in the punisher, too. These mental states are not conducive to learning (unless you *want* the subject to learn fear, anger, and hatred, emotions that are sometimes deliberately established in the training of terrorists).

One reason we keep thinking punishment works is that sometimes—if the subject understands which action is being punished, if the motivation for doing the behavior is small, if the fear of future punishment is large, and finally, if the subject can control the behavior in the first place (punishment doesn't cure bed-wetting, for example)—the punished behavior stops. A child who is scolded severely the first time he or she crayons on the wall may very well stop defacing the house. A citizen who cheats on his income tax and gets fined for it may not try it again.

Punishment has the best chance of halting a behavior in its tracks if the behavior is caught early, so that it has not become an established habit, and if punishment itself is a novel experience for the subject, a shock to which the person or animal has not become hardened.

My parents punished me exactly twice in my whole upbringing (and then only with scoldings), once at age six for pilfering, and once at age fifteen for skipping school and causing everyone to think I'd been abducted. The extreme rarity of the punishment experience contributed vastly to the effect. Both behaviors stopped instantly.

If you are going to use punishment, you may want to arrange things so that the subject sees the aversive as a consequence of its own acts, and not as something associated with you. Suppose you have a large hairy dog that likes to sleep on the couch, and you don't want it doing that. Punishment—scolding and so on—may keep the dog off the couch when you are there, but not when you are absent. One old training trick is to set a few small mousetraps and put them on the couch: punishment in absentia. Then, when the dog jumps up, the mousetraps go off, startling and perhaps pinching him. The mousetraps punish jumping on the couch. This event also negatively reinforces, or strengthens, the behavior of staying on the floor in order to avoid mousetraps. The dog's own action triggered the aversive event, and one bad experience can be sufficient to eliminate the behavior of sneaking onto the couch. I hasten to add that this is likely to work with some dogs but not others. One boxer owner reported that his dog, faced with mousetraps for the second time, dragged a blanket down from the back of the couch onto the mousetraps, set off the traps, and then lay on the blanket on the couch.

When a punishment does effectively halt a behavior, that sequence of events is very reinforcing for the punisher. The punisher tends then to sally forth confidently to punish again. It always surprises me to witness the great faith that arises, in some individuals, in the effectiveness of punishment. I have seen it exhibited and defended by disciplinarian schoolteachers, bullying athletic coaches, domineering bosses, and well-intentioned parents. Their own punishing behavior may be maintained by a meager handful of successes in a morass of not-so-good results and can persist despite logical evidence to the contrary—despite the presence of other teachers in the same school, other coaches, heads of other businesses, other generals, presidents, or parents who can be seen to be getting results that are just as good or better without using punishment at all.

Punishment often constitutes revenge. The punisher may not really care whether the victim's behavior changes or not; he or she is just getting revenge, sometimes not against the recipient but against society at large. Think of obdurate clerks who, with concealed glee, delay or prevent you from getting your license, your loan, or your library pass over some minor technicality; you get punished and they get even.

Punishing is also reinforcing for the punisher because it demonstrates and helps to maintain dominance. Until the day when a boy is big enough to hit his brutal father back, the father feels dominant and is in truth the dominant one. This in fact may be the main motivation behind our human tendency to punish: establishing and maintaining dominance. The punisher may be primarily interested not in behavior but in being proved to be of higher status.

Dominance hierarchies and dominance disputes and testing are a fundamental characteristic of all social groups, from flocks of geese to human governments. But perhaps only we humans learn to use punishment primarily to gain for ourselves the reward of being dominant. So think, when you are tempted to punish: Do you want the dog, the child, the spouse, the employee to alter a given behavior? In that case, it's a training problem, and you need to be aware of the weaknesses of punishment as a training device. Or do you really want revenge? In that case you should seek more wholesome reinforcers for yourself.

Or perhaps you really want the dog, the child, the spouse, the employee, the neighboring nation, and so on to stop disobeying you. In whatever manifestation, do you want the subject to stop going against your superior will and judgment? In that case it's a dominance dispute, and you're on your own.

Guilt and shame are forms of self-inflicted punishment. Almost no sensation is more disagreeable than the clammy hand of guilt closing around one's heart; it is a punisher that only the human race could have invented. Some animals—dogs, certainly—can show embarrassment. But none, I think, waste time suffering from guilt over actions in the past.

The amount of guilt we deal out to ourselves varies hugely. One person can feel relaxed and justified after committing a major crime while another feels guilty over chewing a stick of gum. Many people do not experience guilt or shame in their daily lives, not because they are perfect, nor because they are unfeeling hedonists, but because they respond to their own behavior in alternative ways. If they do something that bothers them in retrospect, then they don't do it again. Others make the same mistake over and over—acting the fool at a party, saying unforgivable words to a loved one—in spite of invariably feeling hellishly guilty the next day.

One would think that fear of feeling guilty would act as a deterrent, but usually at the moment we are doing the deed that will later cause guilt, we are feeling impeccably fearless. As a way of changing behavior, guilt ranks right along with flogging or any other form of delayed punishment—it is not very effective.

Therefore, if you are a person who punishes yourself in this way (and most of us are, having been taught to do so in early childhood), you should recognize that it is a Method 2 solution and not necessarily something you deserve. You might have good reasons to want to get rid of the behavior that makes you feel guilty, but you might then have much better luck with some method or combination of methods other than self-punishment.

Method 3: Negative Reinforcement

A negative reinforcer is any unpleasant event or stimulus, no matter how mild, that can be halted or avoided by changing one's behavior. A cow in a field with an electrified fence touches her nose to the fence, feels a shock, and pulls back, which stops the shock. She learns to avoid the shock by not touching the fence. While touching the fence has been punished, the behavior of avoiding the fence has been reinforced, by a negative rather than positive reinforcer.

Life abounds in negative reinforcers. We shift position when a chair gets uncomfortable. We know enough to come in out of the rain. Some people find the smell of garlic appetizing, and others find it offensive. The stimulus becomes a negative reinforcer only if it is perceived as unpleasant by the recipient and if the behavior is modified—shifting seats on the bus, away from a garlic-eater, say—to remove the unpleasantness.

As we saw in Chapter 1, almost all traditional animal training consists of the applied use of negative reinforcers. The horse learns to turn left when the left rein is pulled, because by doing so it can ameliorate the tugging feeling in the left corner of its mouth. Elephants, oxen, camels, and other beasts of burden learn to move forward, halt, pull loads, and so on to avoid the tug of a halter, the poke or blow of a prod, goad, or whip.

Negative reinforcement can be used to shape behavior. As with positive reinforcement, the reinforcer must be contingent upon the behavior; one must cease "prodding" when the response is correct. Unfortunately, because the prodding, in whatever form, results in a change in behavior, the behavior of the person doing the prodding may be positively reinforced, so that, as with punishing, the tendency to lay on with the aversives increases. Naggers, for example, may eventually get results, and this is reinforcing to the nagger. So nagging escalates, sometimes so much that the nagger goes on nagging whether the desired response has occurred or not. Think of the mother in *Portnoy's Complaint* who complains, while her son is visiting, "We never see you!"

Positive and negative reinforcement contingencies are often reciprocal. Behaviorist Myrna Libby, Ph.D., gave me this example: A child is tantruming in the store for candy. The parent gives in and lets the child have a candy bar. The tantruming is positively reinforced by the candy, but the more powerful event is that the parent is negatively reinforced for giving in, since the public tantrum, so aversive and embarrassing for the parent, actually stopped.

Tantrums can become part of a vicious circle. The parent will go to all kinds of lengths—soothing, protesting, arguing, and reinforcing—to stop a tantrum. So the tantrums escalate, and because they do, the parent's inadvertently reinforcing efforts escalate as well. I know of one household in which a child threw a full-blown, fifteen- or twenty-minute screaming tantrum nearly every night, just at dinnertime. Both the child's behavior and the parents' anxious responses were so strongly maintained, by interlocking positive and negative reinforcements, that the behavior continued for over three years.

People use spontaneous negative reinforcers on each other all the time: the warning glance, the frown, the disapproving remark. Some children's lives, and some spouses' lives too, are filled with constant daily effort to behave in such a way as to avoid disapproval. The overpunished child may become hostile, evasive, and a punisher himself in adulthood. In contrast, the child that grows up striving not to please, exactly, but to bring a halt, if only temporarily, to chronic disapproval, may become timid, self-doubting, and anxious in adult life. A therapist specializing in phobic patients tells me that her clients, with their crippling irrational fears of crowds or elevators, were all raised on a steady diet of negative reinforcement.

Since one *can* use negative reinforcement effectively to shape improved behavior, as with punishment, the experience can reinforce the trainer's willingness to use coercion. As Murray Sidman, Ph.D., has observed to me, "A few successful applications of even mild negative reinforcement may turn a trainer into an invariable user of negative reinforcement."

However, because negative reinforcers are aversive—something the subject wants to avoid—every instance of their use contains a punisher. Pull on the left rein, and you are punishing going straight ahead, as well as negatively reinforcing turning to the left when that occurs. The traditional trainer typically doesn't think of his negative reinforcers—his reins or choke chains or verbal corrections—as punishment. After all, trainers explain, these tools are gently used, on the whole: if the trainer really wanted to punish, there are much more severe corrections available. And, the argument typically continues, if you use a lot of praise and positive reinforcers as well, no harm is done in the long run.

However, the strength of the aversive can only be judged by the recipient. What the trainer may consider to be mild may be seen by the trainee as blisteringly severe. Furthermore, since all negative reinforcement, by definition, includes a punisher, making a practice of using negative reinforcement puts you at risk for all the unpredictable fallout of punishment: avoidance, secrecy, fear, confusion, resistance, passivity, and reduced initiative, as well as spillover associations, in which anything that happens to be around, including the training environment and the trainer, becomes distasteful or disliked, something to be avoided or even fled from.

Because training with negative reinforcers or correction is the traditional and conventional system, the resulting fallout is extraordinarily obvious once you look for it. I have attended national-level dog obedience competitions and been startled by the glum faces, unwagged tails, and cautious, inhibited movements of many of the top-level performance dogs. Go to any riding academy or horseback event, and ask yourself if the horses look cheerful. Most people, even professional equestrians, and even those who consider themselves to be modern and humane trainers, don't know what a happy-eyed horse looks like. They've never seen one.

Negative reinforcers can be benign, as illustrated earlier in the matter of the shy llama. My daughter's dog is affectionate and likes to lick the baby's face. The baby, a year old, likes the dog but doesn't like having his face washed. He has learned that if he puts his hands out and squawks, the dog will stop. Now when the dog approaches, tail wagging, the baby produces his baby version of "No way!" and the lick is forestalled. The baby is quite happy with his new behavior and sometimes tries it (less effectively) on parents and siblings.

But on the whole, babies are one class of organisms for which negative reinforcement is an inappropriate teaching mechanism. It's difficult to discourage a baby from doing what she needs and wants to do by arranging aversive contingencies. Babies don't understand time-outs and scoldings. The crawler reaching for the bric-a-brac on Grandma's coffee table is most likely to ignore the warning "No!" and to wail—but keep right on reaching—if her hands are smacked. It's far better to use Method 8 (Change the motivation) by putting the objects out of reach, or Method 5

(Train an incompatible behavior) by giving the baby something else to play with—or both. Babies are not programmed to learn easily to avoid aversives, though they can learn rapidly through positive reinforcement. One might say that babies are born to please, not to obey.

Baby animals also tend to learn more easily through positive reinforcement and to be bewildered and frightened by punishment and negative reinforcers. Conventional dog trainers usually do not advise formal obedience training until a dog is six months of age. The reason they give is that the puppy is too young to learn; but the real problem is that formal training is generally aversive, and the puppy is too young to learn that particular way. With praise and petting and food, you can teach a puppy almost anything, starting even before weaning, but put a choke chain on it and try to force it to heel, sit, or stay, and you will cow and frighten the puppy before you can teach it much.

There is another class of subjects that are singularly unamenable to negative reinforcement: wild animals. Anyone who has ever kept a wild pet—an ocelot, a wolf, a raccoon, an otter—knows that they don't take orders. It is extraordinarily difficult, for example, to teach a wolf to walk on a leash, even if you have raised it from puppyhood and it is quite tame. If you pull, it pulls back automatically, and if you are too insistent and pull too hard, the wolf, no matter how calm and sociable it usually is, panics and tries to escape.

Put a tame pet otter on a leash, and either you go where the otter wants to go, or it fights the leash with all its might. There seems to be no middle ground where a little tug might be used to shape compliance.

Dolphins are the same. For all their vaunted trainability, they either resist or flee any kind of force. Push a dolphin, and it pushes back. Try to herd dolphins from one tank to another with nets; if they feel crowded, bold individuals will charge the net and timid ones will sink to the tank bottom in helpless fear. You have to shape the behavior, with positive reinforcers, of moving quietly ahead of the net; and even if you have done that, almost

SAMPLES OF METHOD 3: NEGATIVE REINFORCEMENT

Negative reinforcement may be effective and the method of choice in some situations. The car device described here works very well, especially if the children are too tired and cross to be amenable to alternatives such as playing games and singing songs (Method 5).

BEHAVIOR	APPROACH
Roommate leaves dirty laundry all over the place.	Disconnect the TV or withhold dinner until the laundry is picked up. (Cease negative reinforcer when compliance is obtained; reinforce even halfhearted efforts at first.)
Dog in yard barks all night.	Shine a strong light on doghouse when dog barks. Turn the light off when the dog stops barking.
Kids too noisy in the car.	When the decibel level meets the pain threshold, pull over and stop the car. Read a book. Ignore arguing about stopping; that's noise, too. Drive on when silence reigns.
Spouse habitually comes home in a bad mood.	Turn your back or leave the room briefly when the tone of his or her voice is disagreeable. Return and give your attention at once when the voice is silent or normal.
Faulty tennis swing.	Have a coach or bystander verbally correct the bad swing ("Ah-ah-ah," or "No!") in midswing each time you do it. Develop another swing that shuts off the correction.

BEHAVIOR	APPROACH
Shirking or lazy employee.	Tighten supervision and rebuke each instance in which work falls below par.
Hating to write thank-you notes.	Negative reinforcement comes automatically from friends and loved ones. Aunt Alice will let you know how worried she is that you never got the scarf, and your family will let you know that you ought to write Aunt Alice. The information will be delivered with definite aversive overtones.
Cat gets on the kitchen table.	Put cellophane tape, sticky side up, on the kitchen table.
Surly bus driver is rude to you and makes you mad.	Stand in the door or near the driver so he can't drive on until you move. Move when he stops talking, even for an instant.
An adult offspring who you think should be self-sufficient wants to move back in with you.	Let the adult child come back, but charge him or her exactly what you would charge a stranger for rent, food, and any additional services such as laundry or babysitting. Make it worthwhile financially to move on.

any netting operation requires one alert human standing by, ready to jump into the water and disentangle an animal that has rushed the net before it drowns.

Psychologist Harry Frank suggests that this resistance to negative reinforcement is a principal difference between wild and domesticated animals. All domesticated animals are susceptible to negative reinforcement—they can be herded, led, shooed, or generally pushed around. We humans, intentionally or accidentally, have selectively bred this characteristic into them. After all, the cow that cannot be herded or shooed, that like a wolf or dolphin either resists the aversive stimulus or panics and flees, is the cow that's going to end up outside the kraal at night and get eaten by lions; or, as a nuisance, it will be the cow most likely to be killed and eaten by the people. Her genes won't stay in the gene pool.

Obedience, whether expressed as a willingness to knuckle under or as a hesitation in the fight-or-flight reaction in which mild negative reinforcement may be used to coerce learning, is built into all of our domestic animals—with one exception. the cat. It is, for example, really hard to teach a cat to walk on a leash; go to a cat show, and you will see that the professionals don't even bother to try—cats are carried or cats are caged, but they are not walked around on leashes.

Harry Frank suggests that this is because the cat is not a true domestic animal and therefore lacks that susceptibility to negative reinforcement. It may, rather, be a commensal, an animal that, like the rat and the cockroach, shares our abodes to its benefit. More probably the cat is a symbiote, an animal that trades favors with us for mutual benefit—food, shelter, and patting from us; mouse catching, entertainment, and purring from the cat. Work and obedience, however, no. Which may explain why some people don't like cats: They fear the uncontrollability.

For all you cat haters out there, there is one punisher that does work with cats and can be used as a negative reinforcer: spraying water at the cat's face. Once at a dinner party where I was wearing a new black wool dress, my hostess's white angora cat repeatedly jumped into my lap. The hostess thought that was cute, but I did not want white cat hairs on my dress. When she was not looking, I dipped my fingers into my wineglass and spritzed the cat in the face. It left at once and never came back: a fine and useful negative reinforcer.

Method 4: Extinction

If you have trained a rat to press a lever repeatedly for a food reward and then you shut off the food-delivering machine, the rat will press the lever a lot at first, then less and less, until it finally gives up. The behavior is "extinguished."

Extinction is a term from the psychology laboratories. It refers to the extinction not of an animal but of a behavior, a behavior that dies down by itself for lack of reinforcement, like a burnt-out candle.

Behavior that produces no results—not good results or bad results, just no results—will probably extinguish. This does not always mean you can ignore a behavior and it will go away. The behavior of ignoring a human being is a result in itself, being such an unsocial thing to do. One cannot always count on extinguishing behavior in another by ignoring it.

If a behavior has been reinforced by attention, ignoring it may work. I once watched Thomas Schippers, the symphony conductor, running a rehearsal of the New York Philharmonic. A ferocious conductor—but a ferocious orchestra, too. As Schippers walked to the podium, the orchestra was being naughty; a woodwind warbled "I wish I was in Dixie," and a violin made an incredibly human "Oh-oh." Schippers ignored the foolery, and it quickly extinguished.

Extinction in human interactions best applies, it seems to me, to verbal behavior—whining, quarreling, teasing, bullying. If these kinds of behavior do not produce results, do not get a rise out of you, they extinguish. Keep in mind that getting someone's goat can be positively reinforcing. The brother who gets his little sister into a fit of rage by teasing her about her hairdo is being reinforced. When you flame up at someone else in the office who is one-upping you, he or she has won.

We often accidentally reinforce the behavior we wish would extinguish. Whining, in children, is a parent-trained behavior. Any child who is tired, hungry, and uncomfortable may whine, like a puppy. The world-class whiner, however, is the child whose parents are such masters of self-control that they can withstand huge amounts of whining before they finally crack and say, "All right, I'll get you the damned ice cream cone; now will you please shut up?" We forget, or do not understand, that the eventual reinforcement maintains the behavior; and the variability of the elapsed time to reinforcement makes for a very durable behavior.

Once I saw a pretty little girl of about six in Bloomingdale's bring her mother, her grandmother, and the whole Bloomingdale's linen department to a complete standstill with a virtuoso display of "But you *said*, you *promised*, I don't wanna" and so forth. As well as I could figure out, the child was tired of shopping, perhaps reasonably so. Or she was just tired, period. She wanted to leave, and she had learned to get what she wanted by whining, which eventually was always reinforced.

What do you do if you happen to be stuck for an afternoon with someone else's whiny child? Here's what I do. The minute the protesting or complaining begins in that telltale nasal tone, I inform the child that whining doesn't work with me. (This usually gives him or her food for thought, since they don't think of it as whining; they think of it as logical or even brilliant persuasion.) When they stop whining, I make haste to reinforce, with praise or a hug. If the child forgets and starts whining again, I can usually stop the behavior with a raised eyebrow or a quelling glance. Actually, whiners are often quite intelligent and make pleasant, even interesting companions when they give up their game and the whining is extinguished.

One of the problems of dealing with behavior that is expressed in words is that we humans have inordinate respect for our language. Words are almost magical. In a situation of being bullied or teased, or when one is being whined at, or perhaps most obviously in a marital fight, we tend to deal with the words said, not with the behavior. "But you *promised*" evokes the response "No, I did not promise," or "I know, but I have to go to Chicago tomorrow, so I can't do what I said; can't you understand that?" and so on forever.

SAMPLES OF METHOD 4: EXTINCTION

Method 4 is not useful for getting rid of well-learned, self-rewarding behavior patterns. It is good, however, for whining, sulking, or teasing. Even small children can learn—and are gratified to discover—that they can stop older children from teasing them merely by not reacting in any way, good or bad.

BEHAVIOR	APPROACH
Roommate leaves dirty laundry all over the place.	Wait for him or her to grow up.
Dog in yard barks all night.	This behavior is self-reinforcing and seldom extinguishes spontaneously.
Kids too noisy in the car.	A certain amount of noise is natural and harmless; let it be, they'll get tired of it.
Spouse habitually comes home in a bad mood.	See to it that his or her harsh words have no results, either good or bad.
Faulty tennis swing.	Work on other strokes, footwork, and so on, and try to let the specific error die down from lack of concentrating on it.
Shirking or lazy employee.	If the misbehavior is a way of getting attention, remove the attention; shirking, however, may be self-reinforcing.
Hating to write thank-you notes.	This behavior generally extinguishes with age. Life becomes so full of onerous chores such as paying bills and doing taxes that mere thank-you notes become relaxation by comparison.

BEHAVIOR	APPROACH
Cat gets on the kitchen table.	Ignore the behavior. It will not go away, but you may succeed in extinguishing your own objections to cat hair in your food.
Surly bus driver is rude to you and makes you mad.	Ignore the driver, pay your fare, and forget it.
An adult offspring who you think should be self-sufficient wants to move back in with you.	Accept it as a temporary measure and expect that the adult child will move out as soon as finances improve or the present crisis is over.

We need to separate the words being said from the behavior. When a husband and wife are fighting, for example, fighting is what is going on. Yet the topic of the fight often steals the show. You can argue each point into the ground, and you can be dead right about the words that are being said (therapists have to listen to miles of replays of such tapes), but you still are not dealing with the behavior—fighting.

In addition to being too easily sucked into the words of a conflict ("He said I'm a coward—I am *not* a coward"), we often fail to notice the very fact that we are reinforcing it. And not just by letting ourselves be trapped into anger. Take the husband who always comes home in a bad mood. The crabbier he is, the faster his wife rushes about to try to please him, right? What is she actually reinforcing? Crabbiness.

A cheerful demeanor, no speeding up of dinner, and an absence of hand wringing and upset on the spouse's part can do a lot to eliminate the usefulness to the crabby one of any display of moodiness or temper. On the other hand, withdrawing into icy silence or screaming back or punishing would all be results and consequently might be reinforcing.

By ignoring the behavior without ignoring the person, you can arrange for many disagreeable displays to extinguish by themselves because there is no result, good or bad. The behavior has become unproductive. Hostility requires a huge amount of energy, and if it doesn't work it is usually quickly abandoned.

Many behaviors are temporarily limited in themselves. When children or dogs or horses are first let out-of-doors after a period of confinement and inactivity, they crave to run and play. If you try to control this, you may have to exert quite a lot of effort. It's often easier just to let them run around for a while, until the urge for action is satiated, before you ask for disciplined behavior or start to train them. Horse trainers call this "getting the bugs out." A wise horse trainer may turn a young horse loose in the ring for a few minutes, to kick and buck and run around, before saddling it and making it get to work. Calisthenics before drill team or football practice serve somewhat the same purpose. In addition to getting the muscles moving, which reduces the chance of strains and injuries, these "gross motor activities" sop up some of the loose energy, so that romping and horseplay extinguish and the troops or players can become more attentive to the training process.

Habituation is a way to eliminate unconditioned responses. If a subject is exposed to an aversive stimulus that it cannot escape or avoid, and which nothing it does has any effect on, eventually its avoidance responses will extinguish. It will stop reacting to the stimulus, pay no attention, and apparently become unaware of it. This is called habituation. In my New York apartment I found the street noise unbearable at first, but eventually, like most New Yorkers, I learned to sleep through the sirens, yelling, garbage trucks, even car crashes. I became habituated. Police horses are sometimes trained by subjecting them to all kinds of harmless but alarming events, such as opening umbrellas, flapping papers, being tapped all over with rattling tin cans, and so on. The horses become so habituated to startling sights and sounds that they remain unflappable no matter what events the city streets have to offer.

Method 5: Train an Incompatible Behavior

Here come the good fairies: the positive methods for getting rid of unwanted behavior.

One elegant method is to train the subject to perform another behavior physically incompatible with the one you don't want.

For example, some people do not like to have dogs begging at the dining-room table. I hate it myself—there is nothing more likely to curb my appetite than doggy breath, sad-dog eyes, and a heavy paw on my knee just as I am lifting a piece of steak to my mouth.

A Method 1 solution is to put the dog outside or shut it in another room during mealtimes. But it is also possible to control begging by training an incompatible behavior—for example, training a dog to lie in the dining-room doorway when people are eating. First you train the dog to lie down, thereby bringing the behavior under stimulus control. You can then make the dog "Go lie down" elsewhere during meals. You reward this behavior with food in the kitchen after the plates are cleared. Going away and lying down is incompatible with begging at the table; a dog cannot physically be two places at once, and so begging is eliminated.

I once saw an orchestra conductor hit on a brilliant use of an incompatible behavior during an opera rehearsal. The whole chorus suddenly fell out of synchrony with the orchestra. It seemed they had memorized one measure of music a beat short. Having identified the problem, the conductor looked for an "s" in the lyrics of that measure, found one, and told the chorus to stress that "s": "The king'sssss coming." It made a funny buzzing sound, but it was incompatible with rushing through the measure too fast, and it solved the problem.

My own first use of Method 5 was in the handling of a potentially very serious dolphin problem. At one time at Sea Life Park we had three kinds of performers in the outdoor show: a group of six dainty little spinner dolphins, a huge female bottlenose named Apo, and a pretty Hawaiian girl who swam and played with the spinner dolphins during part of the show. Contrary to popular opinion, dolphins are not always friendly, and bottlenoses in particular are apt to bully and tease. Apo, the six-hundred-pound bottlenose, took to harassing the swimmer when she got in the water, dashing under her and boosting her into the air, or slapping her on the head with her tail flukes. It terrified the girl, and it was indeed very dangerous.

We did not want to take Apo out of the show, since her leaps and flips made her its star. We started constructing a pen in which she could be shut during the swimmer's performance—a Method 1 solution—but meanwhile we trained an incompatible behavior. We got Apo to press on an underwater lever, at the pool's edge, in return for fish rewards.

Apo enthusiastically learned to press the lever repeatedly for each fish; she even took to defending her lever from other dolphins. During shows a trainer put Apo's lever in the pool and reinforced lever pressing whenever the swimmer was out in midwater playing with the spinners. Apo could not press her lever and simultaneously be in the middle of the pool beating up the swimmer; the two behaviors were incompatible. Fortunately Apo preferred lever pressing to swimmer harassment, so the behavior was eliminated. (The swimmer, however, never quite trusted this magic and calmed down completely only when Apo was back safely behind bars.)

Training an incompatible behavior is a good way to attack a faulty tennis swing or any other muscular pattern that has been learned wrong. Muscles "learn" slowly but well; once something has become part of your movement patterns it is hard to unlearn. (Piano lessons were frustrating to me as a child because it seemed in every piece my fingers would learn one note wrong and stumble in the same place every time.) One way to deal with this is to train an incompatible behavior. Using a tennis swing as an example, first take the movement apart in your mind—posture, position, footwork, start, middle, and end—and go very slowly through each portion of the movement, or many times through just one portion

SAMPLES OF METHOD 5:
TRAIN AN INCOMPATIBLE BEHAVIOR

Sensible people often employ this method. Singing and playing games in the car relieves parents as well as children from boredom. Diversion, distraction, and pleasant occupations are good alternatives during many tense moments.

BEHAVIOR	APPROACH
Roommate leaves dirty laundry all over the place	Buy a laundry hamper and reward the roommate for placing laundry in it. Wash laundry together, making it a social occasion, when the hamper is full. Laundry care is incompatible with laundry neglect.
Dog in yard barks all night	Train it to lie down on command; dogs, like most of us, seldom bark lying down. Yell the command out the window or rig an intercom to the doghouse. Reward with praise
Kids too noisy in the car.	Sing songs, tell stories, play games: "Ghost," "I Spy with My Little Eye," "20 Questions," "Found a Peanut," and so on. Even three-year-olds can sing "Found a Peanut " Incompatible with squabbling and yelling.
Spouse habitually comes home in a bad mood.	Institute some pleasant activity on homecoming, incompatible with grouching, such as playing with the children or working on a hobby. Thirty minutes of total privacy is often good. Spouse may need time to unwind before switching to family life

BEHAVIOR	APPROACH
Faulty tennis swing.	Train an alternative tennis swing from scratch (see text).
Shirking or lazy employee.	Order him or her to work quicker or harder on a specific task; watch, and praise the job on completion.
Hating to write thank-you notes	Train some replacement behavior: If someone sends you a check, write a few grateful words on the back as you endorse it—the bank will take care of the rest. For other kinds of presents, call the sender that very night and say thank you. Then you will never have to write a letter.
Cat gets on the kitchen table.	Train the cat to sit on a kitchen chair for petting and food reward. An eager or hungry cat may hit that chair so hard it slides halfway across the kitchen, but still the cat is where you want it, not on the table.
Surly bus driver is rude to you and makes you mad.	Respond to snarls or bullying with eye contact, a civil smile, and an appropriate social remark—"Good morning"—or, if the driver is really scolding you, with sympathy: "You must have a hard job!" This sometimes prompts courtesy in return, which you can then reinforce.
An adult offspring who you think should be self-sufficient wants to move back in with you.	Help him or her to find another place to live, even if you have to pay for it at first.

if necessary. Train a completely different swing, a set of new motions. When the muscles begin to learn the new pattern, you can put it together and speed it up.

When you start using it in playing time, at full speed, you must pay absolutely no attention at first to where the ball goes; just practice the movement pattern Now you should have two swings—the old faulty one and the new one. The two are incompatible; you cannot make two swings at once. But while you may never get rid of the old pattern completely, you can reduce it to a minimum by replacing it with the new one. Once that pattern has become a muscle habit, you can concentrate again on where the ball goes. And presumably, with a better swing, the ball will behave better too. (This is also how I could have tackled my piano-lesson problem.)

Training an incompatible behavior is quite useful in modifying your own behavior, especially when dealing with emotional states such as grief, anxiety, and loneliness. Some behaviors are totally incompatible with self-pity: dancing, choral singing, or any highly kinetic motor activity, even running. You cannot engage in them and wallow in misery simultaneously. Feeling awful? Try Method 5.

Method 6: Put the Behavior on Cue

This one's a dilly. It works in some circumstances when nothing else will suffice.

It is an axiom of learning theory that when a behavior is brought under stimulus control—that is, when the organism learns to offer the behavior in response to some kind of cue and only then—the behavior tends to extinguish in the absence of the cue. You can use this natural law to get rid of all kinds of things you don't want, simply by bringing the behavior under the control of a cue . . . and then never giving the cue.

I first discovered the use of this elegant method while training a dolphin to wear blindfolds. We wanted to give a demonstration of dolphin sonar, or echolocation, in our public shows at Sea Life Park. I intended to train a male bottlenose dolphin named Makua to wear rubber suction cups over his eyes and then, temporarily blinded, to locate and retrieve objects underwater using his echolocation system. The behavior has become a standard item in oceanarium shows nowadays.

The blindfolds didn't hurt Makua, but he didn't care for them. By and by, when he saw the suction cups in my hands, he took to sinking to the bottom of the tank and staying there. He would lie there for up to five minutes at a time, waving his tail gently and watching me up through the water with a "Gotcha!" look in his eye.

I judged it would be unprofitable to try to scare or poke him up to the surface, and foolish to bribe or lure him. So one day, when he sank on me, I rewarded him with the whistle and a bunch of fish. Makua emitted a "surprise bubble"—a basketball-sized sphere of air which, in the dolphin world, means "Huh?"—and came up and ate his fish. Soon he was sinking on purpose, to earn reinforcers.

Then I introduced an underwater sound as a cue and reinforced him only for sinking on cue. Sure enough, he stopped sinking in the absence of the cue. Sinking was never a problem again; when I went back to blindfold training, he accepted his blindfolds like a trouper.

I have also used this method to calm down noisy kids in the car. If you are on your way to someplace wonderful—the circus, say—the children may be noisy because they are excited, too excited to be amenable to Method 5, playing games and singing songs. And on a happy occasion you don't want to use Method 3, negative reinforcement, by pulling over and stopping the car until they are quiet. Now Method 6 is useful: Bring the behavior under stimulus control. "Okay, everybody make as much noise as you possibly can, starting *now*!" (You make noise, too.) This is a lot of fun for about thirty seconds, and then it palls. Two or three repetitions are usually more than enough to ensure reasonable

SAMPLES OF METHOD 6:
PUT THE BEHAVIOR ON CUE

It doesn't seem logical that this method would work, but it can be startlingly effective, and sometimes almost an instantaneous cure.

BEHAVIOR	APPROACH
Roommate leaves dirty laundry all over the place.	Have a laundry fight. See how big a mess you can both make in ten minutes. (Effective; sometimes the untidy person, seeing what a big mess looks like, is then able to recognize and tidy up smaller messes—one shirt, two socks—that may still bother you but were previously not perceived as messy by the roommate.)
Dog in yard barks all night.	Train the dog to bark on command "Speak!" for a food reward. In the absence of the command, no point in barking.
Kids too noisy in the car.	Put noisemaking under stimulus control (see text).
Spouse habitually comes home in a bad mood.	Set a time and a signal for grouching; sit down for ten minutes, say, starting at 5 P.M. During that period reinforce all complaining with your full attention and sympathy. Ignore complaining before and after.
Faulty tennis swing.	If you told yourself to hit the ball wrong, and learned to do it on purpose, would the fault tend to extinguish when you did not give the command? It might.

BEHAVIOR	APPROACH
Shirking or lazy employee.	Order up goof-off time. This was an amazingly effective technique used by the president of an ad agency where I once worked.
Hating to write thank-you notes.	Buy a memo pad, notepaper, stamps, a pen, an address book, and a red box. Put the supplies inside the box. When you get a present, write the donor's name on the memo pad, put it on the box, put the red box on your pillow or dinner plate, and don't sleep or eat until you've obeyed the cue of the box and written the letter and sealed, stamped, and mailed it
Cat gets on the kitchen table.	Train it to jump up on the table on cue and also to jump down on cue (this impresses guests). You can then shape the length of time it has to wait for the cue (all day, eventually).
Surly bus driver is rude to you and makes you mad.	Putting this behavior on cue is not recommended.
An adult offspring who you think should be self-sufficient wants to move back in with you.	As soon as adult children leave home for good, invite them back for visits, making it clear that they should come only by your invitation. Then don't invite them to move in.

quiet for the rest of the ride. You could say that being noisy on cue takes the fun out of it; or you could say that behavior occurring under stimulus control tends to extinguish in the absence of the stimulus. Maybe something more, but this works.

Deborah Skinner, daughter of psychologist B. F. Skinner, passed on to me a splendid use of Method 6 to control dogs crying at the door. She had a small dog that, when shut outside, would bark and whine at the back door instead of going off and relieving itself. Deborah made a small cardboard disk, one side black and the other white, that she hung on the outside door handle. When the black side was out, no amount of yapping would make the people inside open the door. When the white side was out, the dog would be let in. The dog quickly learned not to bother trying to get back in on the black cue. When Deborah judged that an appropriate amount of time had passed she would open the door a crack, turn the cue around, then let the dog in as soon as it asked.

I tried Deborah's doorknob cue when my daughter acquired a toy poodle puppy. Peter was a very small dog, barely six inches high at two months, and it really was not safe to let him run around loose even indoors with no one to watch him. When I was busy and Gale was at school, I shut him in Gale's room, with food, water, newspapers, and a blanket.

Of course when he was shut up alone, he made a terrible racket. I decided to try Deborah's trick by providing a signal for when barking would and would not be responded to. I grabbed the nearest thing—a small towel—and hung it on the inside doorknob. When the towel was there, no amount of yapping would produce results. When the towel was removed, the puppy's calls for company and freedom would be answered.

The puppy caught on right away and gave up agitating when the towel was on the doorknob. The only thing I had to remember in order to maintain the behavior was not to just let the puppy out when I felt like doing so, but to open the door, remove the towel, close the door, wait till the puppy barked, and *then* let him out, thus keeping the barking behavior under stimulus control (in this case, "no towel" being the signal for barking-will-be-rewarded), and thus also keeping all other barking extinguished.

It worked splendidly—for three days. Then one morning Peter's noisy demands were suddenly heard anew. I opened the door and discovered that he had figured out how to leap up, with all his tiny might, and jerk the towel off the doorknob. Once the towel was on the floor, he felt perfectly free to call for release.

Method 7: Shape the Absence of the Behavior

This is a useful technique in cases where you don't have anything particular that you wish the subject to do, just that you want him to stop what he is doing. Example: complaining, guilt-engendering phone calls from relatives whom you like and don't wish to hurt by Method 1, hanging up, or by Methods 2 or 3, scolding or ridicule. The technical term for Method 7 is DRO (Differential Reinforcement of Other behavior).

Animal psychologist Harry Frank, who was socializing wolf pups by bringing them into the house for daily visits, decided to reinforce, with petting and attention, anything that was not in the category of destroying property. It turned out that about the only pastime in a human household that did not involve the pups' chewing up couches, telephone wires, rugs, and so on was lying on the bed; in due course evenings were passed peacefully with Harry, his wife, and three increasingly large young wolves lying on the family bed, watching the nightly news. Method 7.

I used Method 7 to change my mother's behavior on the telephone. An invalid for some years, my mother lived in a nursing home. I visited her when I could, but most of our communication took place on the telephone. For years, these phone calls were a trouble to me. The conversations were usually, and sometimes exclusively, concerned with my mother's problems—pain, loneliness, lack of money: real problems I was powerless to mitigate.

SAMPLES OF METHOD 7: SHAPE THE ABSENCE OF UNWANTED BEHAVIORS

This takes some conscious effort over a period of time, but is often the best way to change deeply ingrained behavior.

BEHAVIOR	APPROACH
Roommate leaves dirty laundry all over the place.	Buy beer or invite over members of the opposite sex whenever quarters are tidy or roommate does the laundry.
Dog in yard barks all night.	Go out and reward him now and then at night when he has been quiet for ten, twenty minutes, an hour, and so on.
Kids too noisy in the car.	Wait for a quiet time and then say "You all have been so quiet today that I'm going to stop at McDonald's." (Say this right near McDonald's so you can keep your promise promptly, before they get noisy again!)
Spouse habitually comes home in a bad mood.	Think up some good reinforcers and surprise him or her with them whenever the mood does happen to be pleasant.
Faulty tennis swing.	Ignore bad shots, and praise yourself for good ones. (This *really* works.)
Shirking or lazy employee.	Praise the hell out of him for any job actually done satisfactorily. (You do not have to keep this up for a lifetime, just long enough to establish the new trend.)

BEHAVIOR	APPROACH
Hating to write thank-you notes.	Treat yourself to a movie any time you get a present and promptly write and mail the thank-you note.
Cat gets on the kitchen table.	Rewarding the cat for periods of staying off the table is practical only if you keep the kitchen door closed when you're not home so the cat can't indulge in the behavior by itself.
Surly bus driver is rude to you and makes you mad.	If you run into the same bus driver on your route every day, a pleasant "good morning" or even a flower, or a soft drink, when he or she is not being rude, should lead to improvement in a week or two.
An adult offspring who you think should be self-sufficient wants to move back in with you.	Reinforce adult children for living away from home when they are doing so. Don't criticize their housekeeping, choice of apartment, decor, or taste in friends, or they may decide you're right, your house is a better place to live.

Her complaints would turn to tears, and tears to accusations—accusations that made me angry. The exchanges were unpleasant, to the extent that I tended to duck the phone calls.

It occurred to me that there might be a better way. I began concentrating on my own behavior during these phone calls. I used Method 4 and Method 7. I deliberately let her complaints and tears extinguish—Method 4—by saying "Ah," and "Hmm," and

"Well, well." No real results, good or bad. I did not hang up, or attack; I let nothing happen. I then reinforced anything and everything that was not a complaint: queries about my children, news from the nursing home, discussion of weather, or books, or friends. These remarks I responded to with enthusiasm. Method 7.

To my astonishment, after twenty years of conflict, within two months the proportion of tears and distress to chat and laughter in our weekly phone calls became reversed. At the start of the phone calls my mother's worries—"Have you mailed a check? Did you talk to the doctor? Would you call my social worker?"—turned into simple requests instead of reiterated grievances. Now the rest of the time became filled with gossip, reminiscing, and jokes.

My mother had been in her youth, and now became again, a fascinating, witty woman. For the remaining years of her life, I really loved talking to her, in person and on the phone.

"Isn't that awfully manipulative?" a psychiatrist friend once asked. Sure. What was happening before to me was awfully manipulative, too. Perhaps some therapist might have persuaded me to deal differently with my mother, or she with me, but perhaps not. How much simpler it seemed to have a clear-cut Method 7 goal. What are you actually reinforcing? Anything but what you don't want.

Method 8: Change the Motivation

Eliminating the motivation for a behavior is often the kindliest and most effective method of all. The person who has enough to eat is not going to steal a loaf of bread.

A common sight I always wince at is the mother whose small child is having a tantrum in the supermarket and who is jerking on the kid's arm to make it hush up. Of course one can empathize—the tantrum is embarrassing, and jerking is a surreptitious way to shock the child into silence, less conspicuous than yelling or smacking. (It's also a good way to dislocate a little child's elbow or shoulder, as any orthopedic surgeon can tell you.) The problem is usually that the child is hungry, and the sight and smell of all that food is too much for it. Very few young mothers have someone to leave the kids with while they market, and working mothers often have to market right before dinnertime, when they themselves are tired and hungry and hence irritable.

The solution is to feed the kids before or while going to the market; any sort of junk food would be preferable to the distressing scenes that upset child, mother, checkout clerks, and everyone else within range.

Some behaviors are self-reinforcing—that is, the very enactment of the behavior is a reinforcement. Gum chewing, smoking, and thumb sucking are examples. The best way to get rid of these behaviors in yourself or another is to change the motivation. I gave up chewing gum as a child because an aunt told me it made girls look cheap, and not looking "cheap" was a lot more important to me than the pleasure of chewing gum. Smokers quit when their motives for smoking are met in other ways or when motivation to stop—fear of cancer, say—outweighs the reinforcers of smoking. Thumb sucking stops when a child's level of confidence is high enough that he or she no longer needs the self-comforting.

To change motivation, one needs to make an accurate estimate of what the motivation is, and we are often very incompetent at that. We love to jump to conclusions: "She hates my guts," "The boss has it in for me," "That kid is just no damned good." Often we don't even understand our own motivations. The whole profession of psychology and psychiatry has arisen in part for that reason.

Even if we have no unhealthy motivations ourselves, we pay a big penalty for this popular misreading of hidden motivation, especially when we must rely on the medical professions. Physical problems, if not blatantly obvious, are all too often assumed to be emotional in origin and are treated as such, without further examination for a real physical cause. I've seen a businessman

SAMPLES OF METHOD 8: CHANGE THE MOTIVATION

If you can find a way to do it, this method always works and is the best of all.

BEHAVIOR	APPROACH
Roommate leaves dirty laundry all over the place	Hire a maid or housekeeper to tidy up and do laundry, so neither you nor the roommate has to cope. This may be the best solution if you are married to this roommate and you both work. Or the messy person could shape the tidy one to be more casual.
Dog in yard barks all night.	Barking dogs are lonely, frightened, and bored. Give exercise and attention by day so that the dog is tired and sleepy at night, or provide another dog to sleep with at night for company. Or bring dog inside.
Kids too noisy in the car.	Escalation of noise and conflict is often due to hunger and fatigue. Provide juice, fruit and cookies, and pillows for comfortable lounging on home-from-school trips. On long journeys all of the above plus ten minutes per hour of stopping and running around outdoors (good for parents too).

BEHAVIOR	APPROACH
Spouse habitually comes home in a bad mood.	Encourage a job change. Feed cheese and crackers or a cup of hot soup right at the door if hunger and fatigue are the motivation. If stress is the problem, a glass of wine, or fresh air and exercise, may be appropriate.
Faulty tennis swing.	Stop trying to beat the world by winning on the tennis court. Play for fun. (Not applicable to world-class tennis players—or is it?)
Shirking or lazy employee.	Pay for work done, not for hours put in. Task-oriented payment is often very effective with non-Western employees. It's the barn-raising principle; everyone works like mad until the known task is completed, and then everyone can leave. Hollywood movies are made this way.
Hating to write thank-you notes.	We dislike this task because it is a behavior chain (see Method 6) and therefore hard to start, especially since there is no good reinforcement at the end (we already have the present!). We also sometimes put it off because we think we have to write a good, clever, or perfect letter. Not true: All the recipient needs to know is that you are grateful for his or her symbol of affection. Fancy words in a thank-you note are no more important than fancy penmanship on a check: On-time delivery is what counts.

BEHAVIOR	APPROACH
Cat gets on the kitchen table.	Why do cats get on the table? (1) to look for food, so put the food away; (2) cats like to lounge in a high place where they can see what's going on. Arrange a shelf or a pedestal higher than the tabletop, close enough so you can pet the cat, and offering a good view of the kitchen, and the cat may well prefer it.
Surly bus driver is rude to you and makes you mad.	Avoid being snarled at on buses by doing *your* job: Have your change ready, know your destination, don't block the aisle, don't mumble questions, try to be sympathetic about traffic tie-ups, and so on. Bus drivers get crabby because bus riders can be such a pain.
An adult offspring who you think should be self-sufficient wants to move back in with you.	Adults with friends, self-esteem, a purpose in life, some kind of work, and a roof over their heads usually don't want to live with or on their parents. Help your kids find the first three as they are growing up, and they'll usually take care of the job and the roof on their own. Then you can all stay friends.

treated with amphetamines so he would stop "feeling" exhausted, when in fact he *was* exhausted from overwork. In a West Coast city, a woman was diagnosed as neurotic and treated with tranquilizers by half a dozen doctors who apparently saw no physical reason for her symptoms. She nearly ended up in a mental hospital before the seventh doctor discovered she was not malingering but in fact was slowly dying of carbon monoxide poisoning due to a leaky furnace in her home. I myself had some doctor I'd never seen before give me a scolding and a prescription for tranquilizers when what was wrong—and I'd told him I thought so— was not an "imaginary" sore throat but an incipient case of the mumps.

Sometimes, of course, the motive really consists of a need for reassurance, and therefore (if the dispenser of relief is perceived as a powerful and believable person) a tranquilizer or even a sugar pill, or placebo, can calm the spirit, lower the blood pressure, and ease symptoms. Holy water and a blessing can do it, too, if you believe they will. The so-called placebo effect also probably helps to keep witch doctors in business. I see nothing wrong with that. The motivation is a need for reassurance, a very genuine need. The trick in any circumstance is to identify the motivation, rather than just jump to conclusions. One way to do that is to notice what actually helps change the behavior and what doesn't.

The message: If you or a friend has a puzzling behavioral problem, think hard about possible motivations. Never forget the possibility of a cause such as hunger, illness, loneliness, or fear. If it is possible to eliminate the underlying cause, and thus eliminate or change the motivation, you've got it made.

MOTIVATION AND DEPRIVATION

Motivation is a huge subject to which scientists have devoted lifetimes of study. By and large it lies outside the scope of this book, but because it has been necessary to discuss motivation as it relates to undesirable behavior, perhaps this is the place to discuss a training device sometimes used to heighten motivation: deprivation. The theory is if an animal is working for positive reinforcement, the more it needs that reinforcer, the harder and more reliably it will work. Laboratory rats and pigeons are often conditioned with food reinforcers. To heighten their motivation, they are fed less food than they would eat on their own. It is customary to give them just enough to keep them at 85 percent of normal body weight. This is called food deprivation.

Deprivation has become such a standard technique in experimental psychology that when I started training, I assumed it was probably a necessity in working with rats and pigeons. Of course we did not use deprivation with dolphins. Our dolphins were given all they would eat whether they'd earned it or not at the end of each day, since dolphins that do not get enough to eat often become sick and die.

It did occur to me in those days that I was using food and social reinforcers with ponies and children, quite successfully, without first having to reduce the baseline supply of love or nourishment to get results. Perhaps food deprivation was necessary only with simpler organisms, such as rats and pigeons? Yet our Sea Life Park trainers were shaping behavior with food reinforcers in pigs, chickens, penguins, even fish and octopi, and no one ever dreamed of making the poor things extra-hungry first.

I still thought deprivation must be necessary in some kinds of training, since it is so widely used—until I ran into Dave Butcher's sea lions. I had never worked with sea lions myself, and my cursory impression was that they worked only for fish and that they were antisocial and bit trainers. I also thought that only young animals were used for training. All the working animals I had ever seen were comparatively small, between one hundred and two hundred pounds, and I knew that sea lions in the wild get quite large.

Dave Butcher, director of training for Sea World in Florida, showed me more than I'd imagined possible. His sea lions worked for social and tactile reinforcers as well as fish, and of course for conditioned reinforcers and on variable schedules as well. Consequently they did not have to be kept hungry in order to make them perform; during and after the day's performances, the sea lions could have all the fish they wanted. One result was that the sea lions were not snarly and crabby, as any hungry animal might be. They were friendly to those humans they knew, and they enjoyed being touched. I was astonished to see trainers on their lunch hour sunbathing in a pile with their sea lions, each young man resting against the ample flank of one sea lion, with the head of another sea lion in his lap. Another result of the discontinuance of food deprivation was that these sea lions grew . . . and grew! Most trained sea lions in the past, Dave speculated, were small not because of youth but because they were stunted. Sea World's performers weigh six, seven, eight hundred pounds. They are very active, not a bit obese, but they are huge, as nature intended. And they work hard. The five or more daily shows are marvelous.

It's my suspicion now that trying to increase motivation by using deprivation of any sort is not only unnecessary but deleterious. Reducing the normal levels of food, attention, company, or anything else a subject likes or needs before training begins—and solely in order to make the reinforcer more powerful by making the subject more needful—is just a poor excuse for bad training. Maybe it has to be used in the laboratory, but in the real world it is good training that creates high motivation, not the other way around.

Getting Rid of Complicated Problems

In the tables in this chapter, I have shown how each of the eight methods might be applied to specific behavioral problems. For some problems there are one or two solutions that are obviously best. For the dog that barks in the night from fear and loneliness, bringing the dog inside or providing it with a companion will usually ensure that it barks only when genuinely alarmed. For other problems, different methods are appropriate at different times. One can keep children from being too noisy in the car in several ways, depending on the circumstances.

There are other behavioral problems, however, that arise from multiple causes, become firmly entrenched, and are not controllable by any single method—stress symptoms such as nail biting, bad habits such as chronic lateness, addictive behaviors such as smoking. These behaviors can be reduced or eliminated by calculated use of the eight methods, but it may take a combination of several methods to bring the behavior to a halt (and again, I am talking about behavioral problems only in reasonably normal subjects, not in mentally ill or damaged subjects).

Let's look at some examples of problems requiring multiple-method approaches.

BITING YOUR NAILS

Nail biting is both a symptom of stress and a diversion that tends to relieve tension momentarily. In animals such activity is called displacement behavior. A dog in a situation of tension—for instance, when being coaxed over to be petted by a stranger—may suddenly sit down and scratch itself. Two horses threatening each other in a dominance conflict may suddenly go through the motions of grazing. Displacement behavior very often consists of self-grooming activities. In animals under conditions of confinement, the behavior may be carried out so repetitiously that it leads to self-mutilation. Birds preen their feathers until they have plucked themselves bare; cats lick a paw until they have created an open wound. Nail biting (and hair pulling, scratching, and other grooming behaviors) can be carried to this extreme in people, and yet even pain does not stop the behavior.

Because the behavior does indeed distract one from stress momentarily, it becomes self-reinforcing and thus very hard to get rid of. In fact, it becomes a habit and can occur even when there is no stress around. Sometimes Method 4 works—extinction. The habit fades away as one grows older and more confident. But that can take years. Method 1—making nail biting impossible by, say, wearing gloves—and Method 2—punishment by guilt or scoldings—will not teach the nail biter an alternative behavior.

Method 3, negative reinforcement—painting the fingernails with something bad-tasting perhaps—is effective only if the habit is fading away anyway. (This goes for thumb sucking, too.)

If you have this habit, the best way to get rid of it is probably to use a combination of all four of the positive methods. First, using Method 5, an incompatible behavior, learn to observe yourself starting to nail-bite, and every time your hand drifts toward your mouth, jump up and do something else. Take four deep breaths. Drink a glass of water. Hop up and down. Stretch. You cannot be nail biting and doing these things at the same time (and all are, in themselves, tension relievers).

Meanwhile, work on Method 8, changing the motivation. Reduce the overall stress in your life. Share your worries with others, who may in fact have solutions. Get more physical exercise, which usually enables one to face problems more easily. You can also shape the absence of behavior (Method 7) by rewarding yourself with a ring or a good manicure as soon as one and then another nail grows enough to be visible (even if you had to bandage a finger to get there at first). And you might also try psychologist Jennifer James's excellent suggestion for putting the behavior on cue: All day long, every time you find yourself starting to bite your nails, write down what is bothering you at the moment. Then every evening sit down at a specific time and bite your nails continuously for twenty minutes while worrying over everything on your list. In due course, you should be able to shape the nail-biting time down to zero, especially if you combine this effort with the other methods above.

CHRONIC LATENESS

People who lead complex, demanding lives sometimes get to places late because they have too much to do and have to try to cram it all in somehow—working mothers, people in new and fast-growing businesses, some doctors, and so on. Other people tend to be late as a general rule, whether they are busy or not.

Since some of the world's busiest people are impeccably punctual, we have to suspect that some of the people who are often late are choosing to be so.

One would think that tardiness would carry its own downfall, in the form of negative reinforcement—you miss half the movie, the party is almost over, the person you keep waiting is furious. But these are apt to be punishers, not negative reinforcers. They punish the behavior of arriving. And habitually late people generally have marvelous excuses prepared, for which they are pleasantly reinforced with forgiveness (which develops their excuse-making skills and in fact reinforces late arriving).

The fastest way to conquer being late is Method 8, changing the motivation. People have many reasons for being late. One is fear: You don't want to be in school, so you dawdle. Another is a bid for sympathy: "Poor little me, I have been saddled with so many responsibilities that I cannot meet my commitments." There is hostile lateness—when you secretly do not wish to be with those people at all—and show-off lateness, when you make it obvious that you have much more important things to do with your time than show up here.

It really doesn't matter what the particular motives are in a given case. To stop being late, all one has to do is change the motivation by deciding that in all circumstances being on time is going to have first priority over any other consideration. Presto! You will never have to run for a plane or miss an appointment again. As a lifelong latecomer, that's how I cured myself. Having made the decision that promptness was now of major importance, I found that answers came automatically to such questions as "Do I have time to get my hair done before the committee meeting?" or "Can I squeeze in one more errand before the dentist?" or "Do I have to leave for the airport now?" The answers are always no, no, and yes. Once in a while I still slip up, but by and large choosing to be on time has made my life enormously easier, and that of family, friends, and colleagues as well.

If changing the motivation is not enough for you, you could

add Method 5, training an incompatible behavior, by aiming at getting places early (bring a book). Or add Method 7, shaping the absence—reinforce yourself, and get your friends to reinforce you, for what in others might be normal but what in you takes special effort, absence of lateness. And try Method 6, putting lateness on cue. Choose some events to which you truly wish to be late, announce that you intend to be late, and then be late. Since behavior occurring on cue tends to extinguish in the absence of the signal, being deliberately late when it's safe to be so may help extinguish being "accidentally" or unconsciously late when you really should be on time.

ADDICTIONS

Addictions to ingested substances—cigarette smoke, alcohol, caffeine, drugs, and so on—have physical effects that tend to keep you hooked whatever you do and to give you nasty withdrawal symptoms if you must go without the substance. But there are huge behavior components to these addictions as well. Some people behave as if addicted, including suffering withdrawal symptoms, to relatively harmless substances such as tea, soda pop, and chocolate, or to pastimes such as running and eating. Some people can turn addictions on and off. Most smokers, for example, find that the urge to smoke hits as regularly as a clock and that they are frantic if they run out of cigarettes. But some Orthodox Jews can smoke heavily six days a week and then abstain completely on the Sabbath without a pang.

In addition to physical symptoms, most addictions provide temporary stress relief, so that they become displacement activities, which makes them doubly hard to eliminate. But because addictions have strong behavioral components, it is conceivable that any addiction problem can be tackled behaviorally by one or more of the eight methods with some possibility of good results.

Almost all addict-rehabilitation programs, from dry-out clinics

to Synanon, rely heavily on Methods 1 and 8. The desired substance is made physically unavailable, and therapy is given to
try to find some other source of satisfaction for the subject—
increased self-esteem, insight, job skills, whatever—to change the
motivation that provides the needfulness. Many treatments also
rely on Method 2, punishment, usually by preaching about lapses
and thus inducing guilt. I once went through a quit-smoking program, which was in fact very helpful, even though I frequently
cheated. When I cheated—smoked someone else's cigarettes at a
tense business meeting, for example—I felt dreadfully guilty; the
next morning I would be practically ill with guilt. But that didn't
stop me the next time; Methods 2 and 3, punishment and negative reinforcement, did not work very well for me. But they do for
some. Weight-loss programs often emphasize not only public
praise for losing pounds but shame in front of the group for gaining, and some people will work to avoid the possibility of that
shame.

A lot of addictive behavior has elements of superstitious behavior. The action—eating, smoking, whatever—has accidentally
gotten hooked to environmental cues that trigger the urge. A time
of day makes you want a drink, the phone rings and you think of
lighting up a cigarette, and so on. Systematic identification of all
these cues, and extinction of the behavior by *not* doing it on each
cue, one cue at a time, is a valuable Method 4 adjunct to getting
rid of an addictive habit. This might mean something simple such
as putting the ashtrays out of sight, or it might involve a whole
change of scenery, a move to a new environment where nothing
constitutes an old familiar trigger cue (cured heroin addicts are
not likely to stay clean if they go right back to life on familiar
streets).

Punishment has been touted as a behavioral method for con-
trolling addiction. Alcoholics, for example, have been wired up
and then given shocks while lifting a glass of liquor, and medicine
exists that will make you vomit if you ingest alcohol. Like most
negative reinforcers, these work well only if there is someone
around to administer them, and preferably unpredictably.

Most addictive behavior doesn't yield very easily to just one method. I think the way to tackle addictive behavior in yourself—and this is one situation where the subject may very well be the most effective trainer—is to study all eight methods and find some way, with the exception of punishment, to engage in frequent application of every single one.

5

Reinforcement in the Real World

In discussing Skinnerian theory, I pointed out that Schopenhauer once said that every original idea is first ridiculed, then vigorously attacked, and finally taken for granted. I think there is a fourth step in the evolution of an idea: The idea is not only accepted, but understood, cherished, and put to work. This is what I see beginning to happen with positive reinforcement, especially among people who have grown up with Skinnerian concepts in the Zeitgeist, in the air around them—people, that is, who have been born since 1950. They take to positive reinforcement and shaping without fear or resistance, as children nowadays take to the computers that their parents may still shrink from. They share techniques with their elders, and they infect those around them with their enthusiasm. Let me give you some examples I find heartening.

Reinforcement in Sports

From my casual observations, the training of most team sports—pro football, for example—continues in the good old Neanderthal tradition: lots of deprivation, punishment, favoritism, and verbal and mental abuse. The training of individual sports, however, seems to be undergoing a revolution. In fact, it was a symptom of that revolution that prompted the writing of this book. At a dinner party in Westchester County, New York, I was seated next to my hostess's tennis pro, a nice young man from Australia. He said to me, "I hear you were a dolphin trainer. Do you know about Skinner and all that?"

"Yes."

"Well, tell me, where can I get a book about Skinner that will help me be a better tennis coach?"

I knew there was no such thing. Why there wasn't continues to be a mystery to me, but I set out to write one, and here it is. Meanwhile, I pondered the amazing fact that this person, and presumably many like him, knew exactly what was needed. It meant there are people out there who already have a grasp of reinforcement training and want to know more about it.

At that time I was living in New York City. Partly for relief from house-pent, sedentary city life, and partly from a trainer's curiosity, I began to take a few lessons in various kinds of physical activities ranging from name-brand exercise classes to squash, sailing, skiing (both downhill and cross-country), figure skating, and dance.

To my surprise, only one of the instructors I worked under (the exercise-class teacher) relied on traditional browbeating and ridicule to elicit behavior. All the rest used well-timed positive reinforcers and often very ingenious shaping procedures. This contrasted sharply with my earlier memories of physical instruction—ballet classes, riding lessons, gym classes at school and college—none of which I shined in, and all of which I feared as much as enjoyed. Take ice skating, for example. I took figure-skating lessons as a child at a large and successful skating school. The instructor showed us what to do, and then we practiced and struggled until we could do it while the instructor corrected our posture and arm positions and exhorted us to try harder. I never could learn my "outside edges"—gliding in a circle to the left, say, with my weight on the outside edge of the left foot. Since that was preliminary to most of the figures, I didn't get very far.

Now I tried a few lessons at a modern skating school in New York, managed by an Olympic coach. The staff used exactly the same methods on adults as on children—no scolding or urging, just instant reinforcement for each accomplishment; and there was plenty of accomplishment. Every single thing a skater needs to know was broken down into easily managed shaping steps, starting with falling down and getting up again. Gliding on one foot? Easy: Shove off from the wall, feet parallel, gliding on two feet; lift one up, ever so briefly, put it down, then lift the other; then do it again, lift a little longer, and so on. In ten minutes the entire beginners' class, including the weak, the wobbly, the very young, and the very old, were gliding on one foot with looks of wild astonishment and elation on their faces.

I didn't even realize that the "crossover" step they'd shaped in my second lesson had cured my childhood balance problems, until I found myself, during the free-skating period after class, sailing around corners blithely on my outside edges. And more! By the third lesson I could do spins, real spins like the skaters on TV, and natty little jump turns I never dreamed of aspiring to in childhood. (These were at first shaped most ingeniously along the wall.) What a revelation. The difficulty in learning such skills is caused not by physical requirements but by the absence of good shaping procedures.

Skiing is another example. The advent of the fiberglass ski and ski boot made skiing possible for the multitudes, not just for the exceptionally athletic. But what gets the multitudes out on the slopes is the teaching methods that use short skis at first and shape each needed behavior (slowing down, turning, and stopping—and of course falling down and getting up) through a series of small, easily accomplished steps marked by positive reinforcers. I went to Aspen, took three skiing lessons, and skied down an entire mountain. The more vigorous in my beginners' class were tackling the intermediate slopes by the end of a week.

There have always been individual teachers who produce rapid results. I think what had changed in the last decade or two is that the principles that produce rapid results are becoming implicit in the standard teaching strategies: "This is the way to teach skiing: Don't yell at them, follow steps one through ten, praise and reinforce accomplishment at each step, and you'll get most of them out on the slopes in three days." When most instructors are using shaping and reinforcement, and consequently getting rapid results, the rest find they have to shift to the new methods just to compete for jobs. If this is happening in every individual sport, it is probably a major contribution to the so-called fitness craze. Learning active skills has become fun.

Reinforcement in Business

In our country labor and management traditionally adopt an adversary position. The idea that everyone is in the same game together has never been particularly popular in American business. General business practice seems to decree that each side try to get as much as possible from the other while giving as little as possible. Of course this is really dumb from a training standpoint, and some managements lean toward other approaches. In the 1960s "sensitivity training" and other social-psychology approaches were popular, to enlighten management about the needs and feelings of coworkers and employees. One can be as enlightened as possible, however, and still not know what to do about an employee problem. The facts of business are that some people have more status and some less, some take orders and some give them. In our country a working situation is, for the most part, *not* like a family, nor should it be. Family-type interpersonal problem solving is therefore inappropriate.

I was interested recently to see, cropping up here and there in business news and publications, a more trainerly approach—ways to use reinforcement that range from the ingenious to the downright brilliant. For example, one management consultant suggests that when part of a group must be laid off, you identify the bottom 10 percent and the top 20 percent. You lay off the poorest performers, but you also make sure to tell the top 20 percent that they are being retained because they're doing such a good job. What a sensible idea. Besides saving your best people some sleepless nights and reinforcing them quite powerfully under the worrisome circumstances, you may be motivating intermediate performers either to seek the reinforcer they can now see is available or to avoid falling into the lowest percentile themselves.

Reinforcers for middle-level, middle-aged managers can consist of more interesting work at their present level instead of promotion, which they may not be able to handle (or may not want, if it involves relocating the family). Cash bonuses for nonsmokers and for quitting smoking are paid by one computer-software company, and for good reason: The products it makes can be damaged by smoke particles. Other reinforcers in widening use include free choice of working hours, the "flextime" system (especially desirable for working mothers), working in self-managed production teams, and being rewarded for getting the job done rather than for putting in the hours. All of these management techniques are designed around what the worker actually finds reinforcing—what works for people, not just for profits.

Programs aimed at cost cutting and work speedups—programs that essentially try to force workers to do not *quite* as bad a job as they are presently doing—are not nearly as effective as programs that help workers to do a better job and then reward them for it. Corporations that use positive reinforcement often see the results on their bottom line. One example is Delta Airlines, which is known for taking very good care of its employees. During the 1981 recession, in spite of operating losses, Delta refused to lay off any of its 37,000 employees. In fact, it gave a companywide 8 percent pay raise. In a long-established climate of positive reinforcement, the employees thought in the same terms; they turned around and reinforced the company by pooling funds and buying it a new airplane, a $30-million Boeing 767.

Reinforcement in the Animal World

Throughout this book I have spoken of the way reinforcement theory has enabled professional animal trainers to establish behaviors in creatures that simply cannot be trained by force: cats, cougars, chickens, birds in the air, whales and dolphins. Training with reinforcement has opened up areas of discovery that I believe we've only begun to explore.

One of the advantages of reinforcement training is that you don't have to think up something for the animal to do and then train it to do that; you can reinforce anything the animal happens to offer and see where it leads. No one dreamed that harbor seals could "talk," but at the New England Aquarium graduate student Betsy Constantine noticed that a rescued harbor seal named Hoover could make humanlike sounds. She shaped Hoover's sounds with fish reinforcers. Soon Hoover was "saying" a number of things.

"Say hello to the lady, Hoover."

Hoover (in a guttural bass voice but very distinctly): "Hiya, honey, h'are yuh."

It's funny to hear, but also of real scientific interest to mammalogists and bioacousticians.

To me as a behavioral biologist the most useful and wonderful aspect of reinforcement training is the window that the training opens up into an animal's mind. It's been fashionable for decades to deny that animals have minds or feelings, and this was probably healthy—it cleared up a lot of superstitions, over-interpretation ("My dog understands every word I say"), and misreading. But then along came the ethologists, spearheaded by Konrad Lorenz, to point out that animals have internal states—

anger, fear, and so on—and that these are signaled by very clear-cut postures, expressions, and movements, which can be recognized and interpreted.

When you can see the subject and the subject can see you, and yet both of you are protected from any physical encounter or bodily harm (perhaps the animal is inside a cage or pen and you are not), then the animal is free to express any internal states the training interaction provokes. Very often the animal begins directing the resulting social behavior at the trainer—in signals ranging from greeting behavior to temper tantrums. Knowing nothing about a particular species but knowing how any subject tends to react to various training events, one can learn more about the nature of a species' social signals in a half hour of training than in a month of watching the animal interact with its own kind. For example, if I see a dolphin jump up in the air and come down with a big splash in a pool of other dolphins, I can only speculate as to why it did that; but if, in a training session, I fail to reinforce something I had previously reinforced every time, and the dolphin jumps up in the air and comes down with a big, directed splash that soaks me from head to toe, I can say with some certainty that at least part of the time it would seem likely that jump-splashes are aggressive displays, and effective ones, too.

One can tell more than that. Engaging a wild animal in some simple shaping procedure can give you a startling glimpse of what might be called species temperament—of how not only that individual but that species tends to tackle the challenges in its environment. Teaching training to my class of keepers at the National Zoo, I used a number of different species as demonstration animals. I stood on my side of the fence, using a whistle as conditioned reinforcer, and tossing in food; the animals moved about freely on their side. The polar bears turned out to be immensely persistent and dogged. One bear which accidentally got reinforced while sitting still took to offering "sitting still" as a response; slavering hopefully, eyes glued to the trainer, it could sit still for half an hour or more, hoping for reinforcement. It seems possible that in an animal which stalks seals on ice floes for a living, this kind of tenacity and patience has important survival value.

I wouldn't have dreamed of going inside the elephant pens at the National Zoo, no matter how docilely the elephants obeyed their regular handlers. But with the help of keeper Jim Jones, I did run a couple of "freestyle" training sessions through the bars with a young Indian female named Shanti. I decided to shape her to throw a Frisbee, starting with retrieving it. Shanti immediately started playing 101 Things to Do with a Frisbee, especially making noise. (Jim told me elephants like to make noise.) Shanti made noise with the Frisbee by holding it in her trunk and banging it on the wall, by rattling it along the bars like a child with a stick, and by putting it on the floor and shuffling it back and forth with her foot. I was already amused. She was fun.

Shanti quickly learned to fetch the Frisbee to me in return for a toot on the whistle and snack from the bucket. She also quickly learned to stand just a *little* bit farther away each time so I had to reach farther in for the Frisbee. When I didn't fall for that, she whopped me on the arm. When Jim and I both yelled at her for that (a sign of disapproval, which elephants respect), she started fetching nicely but pretended she'd forgotten how to pick up carrots. It took her a full minute, feeling the carrot in my hand with her trunk, while looking meaningfully into my bucket, to get me to understand that she preferred the apples and sweet potatoes that were also in there.

When I proved to be intelligent and biddable in this matter and started giving her the preferred reinforcers, she immediately used the same technique—feeling with the trunk tip while making meaningful glances and eye contact—to try to get me to open the padlock on her cage. Elephants are not just a little bit smart; elephants are eerily smart.

Species temperament shows up in many, many species in a shaping session. When I inadvertently failed to reinforce a hyena, instead of getting mad or quitting, it turned on the charm, sitting down in front of me, grinning and chuckling like a fur-covered

Johnny Carson. In shaping a wolf to go around a bush in its yard, I made the same mistake, failing to reinforce it when I should have; the wolf looked over its shoulder, made eye contact with a long, thoughtful stare, then ran on, right around the bush, earning all the kibble I had in my pocket; it had sized up the situation, perhaps deciding that I was still in the game since I was still watching, and it had taken a chance and guessed at what would work. Big risk takers, wolves. If hyenas are comedians, wolves are Vikings.

Sometimes the animals understand reinforcement perfectly. Melanie Bond, in charge of the National Zoo's great apes, had started reinforcing Ham, the chimpanzee, for various behaviors. One morning he was accumulating his food rather than eating it, with the intention, Melanie supposed, of eating outdoors. When Ham saw that at last Melanie was going over to open the door and let him outside, he knew what to do: He handed her a stalk of celery.

I can sympathize with biologists who want to observe the natural behavior of animals without disturbing or interfering with that behavior in any way, and who thus reject gross interference such as training. And I can understand, though I do not sympathize with, the experimental psychologist who shuns any conclusions about animals that are purely observational and cannot be backed up by numerical data. But I remain convinced that shaping sessions offer a fruitful way to combine both approaches and that both field and laboratory workers who can't or don't consider this tool may be missing a bet.

Shaping and reinforcement, deftly used, may also be of enormous importance in gaining insight into otherwise impenetrable human minds. My friend Beverly worked as a therapist in an institution for multiply handicapped children—children both deaf and blind or paralyzed and retarded. She constructed a device that made patterns of colored lights in response to sounds made into a microphone. Debbie, a paralyzed and retarded victim of cerebral palsy, who lay listless and motionless in bed day and night, laughed when she first saw the lights. She heard her voice amplified, saw the lights increase, and immediately learned that she could make the lights dance herself by continuing to laugh and vocalize. This discovery, that she, Debbie, could cause an interesting event to happen, made it possible for the therapist to begin to teach Debbie to communicate. Another child, born with part of his skull missing and forced to wear a helmet at all times, had always been assumed to be totally blind, since he felt his way from spot to spot and failed to respond to any visual stimuli. Beverly was encouraging him to vocalize into her microphone for the reinforcement of hearing his own voice amplified. Then she realized the boy was orienting to the flickering colored lights, too—and vocalizing longer and longer to make the colors dance. He could see just fine. Once the staff knew that, they had a whole new "channel" through which this child might be reached and helped.

In an institutional setting this particular training toy ended up in a closet. Beverly had only a master's degree and was not expected to initiate innovative therapy. There were no research papers proving that the multiply handicapped could be helped with colored lights, and indeed the departure from established protocol was resented by other staff members. That is not the point. The point is that reinforcement training can provide a lot of illumination—not only to the subject but about the subject—and sometimes in just a few moments of training time.

Reinforcement and Society

It sometimes seems to other people as if the behaviorists are preaching that everything in human behavior is a product of learning and conditioning, and that every human ill, from wars to warts, can be cured with proper use of reinforcement. This is, of course, not so. Behavior is a rich soup of external and internal responses, learned and unlearned. Individuality is inborn, as every mother knows. (The biologist T. C. Schneirla demonstrated individual behavior even in insects.) Furthermore, a tremendous amount of what we do and feel is a product of our evolution as social animals. This includes our tendencies to cooperate and be good to each other ("reciprocal altruism") as well as our tendencies to react aggressively if someone tromps on our ideas or property ("territoriality"). And then what one does or says at a given moment may depend just as much on one's physical state as on past experience or future expectations. A person who is extremely hungry or has a bad cold may behave quite differently from the same person when comfortable, regardless of what else is going on.

So reinforcement has limitations, and I see nothing wrong with that. I envision our understanding of behavior as resembling three interlocking rings. In one ring are the behaviorists such as Skinner and everything we know about learning and the acquisition of behavior; in another ring are the ethologists such as Lorenz and everything we know about the biological evolution of behavior; and in the third ring is behavior we don't yet understand well, such as play. And each ring shares part of its contents by overlapping with the other two.

Since society does not consist entirely of exchanges of reinforcers, social experiments involving reinforcement in group settings have produced mixed results. For example, the use of reinforcers in a structured society—a prison, hospital, or detention home, say—may be undermined by the very people doing the reinforcing. A psychologist friend has described to me a token reinforcement system with juvenile offenders in detention that worked wonderfully in a pilot project but fell apart completely, even producing dissension and rebellion, when established at another institution. It turned out the people in charge were distributing reinforcers as instructed for classroom attendance and other desirable behavior, but they didn't smile when they handed out the tokens. And with that small lapse, which was regarded (and rightly, I think) as an insult by the macho young offenders, the whole effort crumbled.

Reinforcement has been used on an individual and group basis to foster not just specific behavior but characteristics of value to society—say, a sense of responsibility. Characteristics usually considered to be "innate" can also be shaped. You can, for example, reinforce creativity. My son Michael, while going to art school and living in a loft in Manhattan, acquired a kitten off the streets and reinforced it for "cuteness," for anything it did that amused him. I don't know how the cat defined that, but it became a most unusual cat—bold, attentive, loyal, and full of delightful surprises well into middle age. At Sea Life Park we shaped creativity with two dolphins—in an experiment that has now been much anthologized—by reinforcing anything the animals did that was novel and had not been reinforced before. Soon the subjects caught on and began "inventing" often quite amusing behaviors. One came up with wackier stuff than the other; on the whole, even in animals, degrees of creativity or imaginativeness can vary from one individual to another. But training "shifts" the curve for everyone, so that *anyone* can increase creativity from whatever baseline he or she began at.

Society, especially in the school system, is sometimes criticized for dampening creativity rather than encouraging it. I think that while such criticism is warranted, it's understandable that society would prefer the status quo. Once those dolphins learned the value of innovating, they became real nuisances, opening gates, stealing props, and inventing mischief. Innovative people are unpredictable by definition, and perhaps society can stand only a certain percentage of these types. If everybody behaved like our creative dolphins, we'd never get anything done. So, very often, individual creativity is discouraged in favor of group norms. Perhaps the courage it takes to defy that trend benefits the innovators who do succeed.

I think the important impact of reinforcement theory on our society will be not to change specific behaviors or institutions but in the effect on individuals of positive reinforcement itself. Reinforcement is information—it's information about what you are doing that is *working*. If we have information about how to get the environment to reinforce us, then we control our environment; we are no longer at its mercy. Indeed, our evolutionary fitness to some extent depends on such success.

So subjects like to learn through reinforcement not for the obvious reason—to get food or other rewards—but because they actually get some control over what is happening. And the reason people like to modify the behavior of others through reinforcement is that the response is so gratifying. Seeing animals brighten up, little kids' eyes shine, people bloom and glow with accomplishment you have helped them achieve, is in itself an extremely powerful reinforcer. One gets absolutely hooked on the experience of getting good results.

A curious but important corollary to training by reinforcement is that it breeds affection in both subject and trainer. When I was at Sea Life Park, it happened several times that an untamed dolphin, having been shaped with a marker signal, the whistle, and food reinforcers, suddenly became quite docile, allowed itself to be petted, and solicited social attention without any effort by us to "hand-tame" it or train it to do so. I have seen this happen with horses, too, sometimes in a single training session, and even with several species of zoo animals that were in no way gentled or made pets of. The animals behave as if they love the trainer.

The trainer rapidly develops an attachment, too. I remember Shanti the elephant and that wolf, D'Artagnan, with respect, and I even have a soft spot for that dunderheaded polar bear. What happens, I believe, is that the success of the training interchange tends to turn the participants into generalized conditioned reinforcers for each other. The trainer is the source of interesting, exciting, rewarding, life-enhancing events for the subject, and the subject's responses are interesting and rewarding for the trainer, so that they really do become attached. Not dependent, just attached. Comrades in the battle of life.

On the level of human interaction, good use of positive reinforcement can have profound effects. It develops and intensifies family feelings, cements friendships, gives children courage, and teaches them to be imaginative and skilled reinforcers in turn. It makes for great sex, for sex, after all, is in part a mutual exchange of positive reinforcers. If two people get really good at reinforcing each other, they are likely to be a happy pair.

Good use of reinforcement does not mean just scattering rewards around indiscriminately or never saying no. People do fall into that misconception. Once, watching a mother pushing a toddler in a stroller down the street, I noticed that every time the baby began to fret, the mother stopped, got out a little bag of healthful snacks—raisins and nuts—and fed the child, although the child did not appear particularly hungry and sometimes pushed her hand away. Trying to do the right thing, she was conscientiously offering reinforcers to the child for fussing. She was also failing to check for rumpled clothes or other discomforts that might have been making the baby fuss in the first place.

None of us will ever be perfect, and I am not proposing that we should be thinking about reinforcement all the time. I am suggesting that a shift to using positive responses in interactions with others, instead of the harshness, argumentativeness, and withdrawal that are the style in many households and organizations, affects not only the individuals involved but, rippling outward, their whole portion of society.

It seems to me that American society is, for all its freedom, a punitive society. We carry a burden of Calvinistic negativeness that colors all our institutions and much of our judgment, no matter what our personal backgrounds. A switch to positive reinforcement can be a startling event. In 1981 a little town in Arizona, desperate to hang on to its good schoolteachers, set up a foundation, raised money locally, and gave cash bonuses to five teachers, selected by faculty and community vote, amounting in some cases to a month's salary. The money was presented at high school graduation, and the teachers got a spontaneous standing ovation from the students, too. By the third year of operation the program seemed to be benefiting students as well as teachers. A typical mixed bag of races, ethnic backgrounds, and rich and poor, the students were by then ranking well above average on national testings.

What I sense as significant in this story is not the method of reinforcing the top teachers, a good idea in itself, but the fact that the event made the wire services and was national news. Switching to positive reinforcement is at this moment in our culture a novel idea. But then, quickly becoming an acceptable idea, it is less often being dismissed as experimental or crackpot.

It may take a generation or two, or three. I suspect that positive reinforcement—because it is now coupled with a body of theory that makes it possible to analyze what happens when things go wrong—is an idea that will over time prove to be too infectious to keep down. Most behaviorists would, I expect, agree with me, wondering only why it's taking so long.

Perhaps what the humanists object to most in behaviorism is the implication that everything in society could and should be run by intent (as much of it is already—but badly run). I think this is a baseless fear. Skinner's imaginary society, Walden Two, set up entirely on contingencies of reinforcement, would not, in my opinion as a biologist, work out. Idealistic societies, in imagination or in practice, sometimes fail to take into account or seek to eliminate such biological facts as status conflict. We are social animals, after all, and as such we must establish dominance hierarchies. Competition within groups for increased status—in *all* channels, not just approved or ordained channels—is absolutely inevitable and in fact performs an important social function: Whether in utopias or herds of horses, the existence of a fully worked-out hierarchy operates to reduce conflict. You know where you stand, so you don't have to keep growling to prove it. I feel that individual and group status, and many other human needs and tendencies, are too complex to be either met or overridden by planned arrangements of reinforcement, at least on a long-term basis.

What bothers the behaviorists, in turn, is their recognition of the many situations in society where proper use of reinforcement principles could be effective and where we stubbornly, stupidly, unceasingly prefer to do it wrong. For instance: giving arms and aid to countries we *hope* will regard us favorably. Come on! Rewarding someone else in hope of gain to oneself doesn't work; it backfires even on the simplest level. ("She only invited me to her party so I'd bring a present; I hate her." "Aunt Tilly's being extraordinarily nice today; wonder what the old bat wants *this* time.") I'm also not sure that our being tough on countries that misbehave is any better. What if they don't care? What if they wanted to get us mad in the first place?

I realize this may be simplistic, but I also think it is simpleminded to go on and *on* behaving as a nation in ways that any clicker trainer can tell you are guaranteed not to work. As a nation, as well as on an individual level, we ought to be continuously asking ourselves the trainer's fundamental question: What am I actually reinforcing?

The laws of reinforcement are powerful tools. But the rule book is far more versatile than some people have supposed, in fact more versatile than some people would like it to be. To be using reinforcement is to be involved in a process of continual change, of continual give-and-take, of continual growth. One becomes aware of the dualistic, two-way nature of this communion. One becomes more aware of others and, inevitably, more aware of oneself. It could be said that training is a process that requires one to be both inside and outside of one's own skin at the same time. Who is the trainer and who is the trained? Both change and both learn.

Some people have seen reinforcement theory as a method of control, of manipulation, of restriction of individuals and society. But societal changes must begin with personal changes— with shifts in what benefits the individual—just as species changes must begin in the individual gene. Social change cannot be dictated from above—at least not for long. (Orwell's *1984* is wrong, biologically.) Living creatures have a right not only to food and shelter but to a reinforcing environment. The use and understanding of reinforcement is an individual experience, which may lead to benefits for all. Far from being constricting, it frees each one of us to experience, be aware of, and enhance not the mechanistic aspects of living but the rich and wonderful diversity of all behavior.

6

Clicker Training: A New Technology

Clicker Training Catches On

When *Don't Shoot the Dog!* was first published in 1984, applied behavior analysis was still not in general use. Thirty years of dolphin training had not led to other applications. The academic community, while successfully using behavior analysis in corporate and institutional settings, had not come up with easily understood ways for untrained people to use their science. But with dog owners it was beginning to be different. Ian Dunbar, D.V.M., a tremendously talented and influential dog behaviorist, had been writing about and teaching noncoercive, behavior-oriented training for pet owners, and he was recommending *Don't Shoot the Dog!*

It was B. F. Skinner himself who first suggested using clickers with dogs, in the 1960s. But I feel that clicker training began in May 1992, with a panel discussion between trainers and scientists at the Association for Behavior Analysis meetings in San Francisco. This was followed a few days later by a "Don't Shoot the Dog!" seminar for 250 dog trainers that I conducted along with dog trainer Gary Wilkes and marine mammal trainer Ingrid Shallenberger. The little plastic clickers Gary had located in a novelty shop made great teaching tools as well as marker signals. People took to them. One dog-training seminar led to others. These public seminars, and the books, videos, and Internet activities they spawned, were, I believe, the start of the clicker-training movement.

The people in the seminar audiences were not necessarily professional trainers, though they might be keen hobbyists. They were attorneys, pilots, law enforcement officers, teachers, computer programmers, business executives, dentists, doctors, and journalists. They were people with lively interests, lots of energy, and an analytical turn of mind. They began teaching others. Soon thousands of people were trying clicker training and taking it farther than we who kicked it off could ever do on our own.

Two young women in Virginia made a video showing how to use the clicker to teach dogs about thirty tricks, ranging from the easy (ring a bell to be let out) to the fiendishly difficult (pass the biscuit from one dog to another). Steve White, a K-9 police officer in Seattle, developed a clicker-training system for training patrol dogs. One of his canine graduates caught three "bad guys" on its first night on the streets (and its tail was wagging the whole time, a characteristic of clicker dogs). Rosemary Besenick, in Texas, began teaching wheelchair-bound clients, some of whom were developmentally disabled as well, to train their own helper dogs. Dog fanciers clicker-trained show-ring behaviors and won at Westminster.

Kathleen Weaver, another police dog trainer and a high-school computer instructor in Texas, established an online discussion list for clicker trainers, and two thousand signed up. Clicker trainers set up websites, exchanging questions and ideas. (See Resources.) Several behavior analysts jumped on board the Internet and helped to solve problems and improve our understanding of the vocabulary of the science. Chief among these was Marian Breland Bailey, a scientist who had been one of Skinner's first graduate students, and her husband Bob. The Baileys lavished time and teaching skills on the Internet clicker community, winning new recognition from their scientific colleagues and a new public audience.

An astronomer in New Mexico, Helix Fairweather, opened a website to maintain an archive of the most important and useful posts on the ever-growing lists: the so-called "keeper" posts. Alexandra Kurland, a riding instructor and horse trainer in upper New York State, developed the application of clicker training for horses—all kinds of horses and all kinds of tasks, including re-training dangerously aggressive horses.

New clicker trainers shared their achievements on the Internet. People with no previous training skills were teaching their dogs how to find the car keys or TV remote, how to bring in the fire-wood, and how to open the refrigerator, select the right drink (the soda, not the salad dressing), close the refrigerator, and bring the drink to the person who asked for it. Then there was the great Internet Hot Dog Challenge: Can you train your dog to retrieve a whole hot dog without eating it? Of course. The real show-offs taught the cheeseburger retrieve as well—though everyone agreed the cheeseburger arrived a bit too slimy for human consumption.

What was happening was a sort of group creation of a new technology: a new application of an existing science. You could never do this physically; you could never, for example, have that many students in one graduate program, or that many thinkers communicating effectively face-to-face. As Canadian clicker trainer Diana Hilliard observed, the Internet gave us a sort of global Manhattan Project: good minds, and a lot of them, working to-gether on one technology.

Long-Term Side-Effects of Clicker Training

Due to the explosion of clicker training, I began to observe some long-term and more general effects of reinforcement training that I couldn't have imagined earlier. In a paper published by the New York Academy of Sciences in 1981, I pointed out that the qualities people attribute to dolphins—playfulness, intelligence, curiosity, friendliness to humans, and so on—are perhaps due not so much to the dolphins themselves as to the way we train them. Now I had the evidence firsthand. Any creature—a dog, a horse, a polar bear, even a fish—that you shape with positive reinforcers and a marker signal becomes playful, intelligent, curious, and interested in you.

What, you don't believe the fish? For video purposes I shaped a cichlid fish (*Astronotus oscellatus*) to swim through a hoop and to follow a target. (The blink of a flashlight made a good marker signal.) While these fish, commonly called oscars, are known for their tameness and intelligence, I'd never seen one go this far. That fish became king of the castle in my house, splashing water and banging its tank lid to attract attention, touching noses with little children through the glass, and threatening visiting dogs by spreading its fins and gills and making attack-feints. It became, to a quite astonishing extent, playful, intelligent, curious, and friendly, for its five-year life, even though it had long been retired from show biz—and got all its food free.

Long-Term Recall

Whatever the species, another long-term effect of clicker training is that behavior, once learned, is not forgotten. Fifteen years ago I knew this was true for the dolphins, but I couldn't be sure it wasn't special to them. Now I know better. One of the most common reactions, when conventional dog trainers switch over to clicker training, is their astonishment at how incredibly well the dogs retain what they've learned. You don't have to keep retraining the behavior and polishing it and brushing it up, the way you do with correction-trained behaviors. Put in the behavior, and it's there forever. I suspect (though no formal data that I know of yet prove it) that this high rate of retention might be one of the fundamental differences not only between training with positive reinforcers and aversives but between training with a marker signal, and training with just primary reinforcers.

Here's one of my favorite examples of long-term retention from a single training episode.[1] One night after dinner, to amuse my cousins' children, I taught their cat to play the piano. With the word *good* as a marker signal and bits of ham as the primary reinforcer, I shaped the behavior of the cat sitting on the piano bench and plunking at the keys with one paw. (With most cats this takes about five minutes. Cats *like* to train people to produce treats predictably.) After that evening no one ever asked the cat to do it again, nor did the cat offer the behavior.

One morning two years later my cousin called to tell me that the previous night they were awakened by ghostly sounds from downstairs: Someone seemed to be playing the piano. On investigation, he found that the living-room doors, as usual, had been shut to conserve heat. And inside the living room, the cat, who normally slept upstairs in the bedroom, was sitting on the piano bench. When, one presumes, the normal responses of meowing and perhaps scratching at the door didn't work, the cat offered a learned behavior to ask, not for food this time, but for its preferred sleeping place. The effort was a success.

Accelerated Learning

Another newly apparent element of clicker training is the acceleration of learning that occurs with it. Competent clicker trainers (some of whom achieve competency almost from the beginning) may accomplish in days behavior that takes months or years to establish by conventional training. The most clear-cut examples I have found so far are in the dog obedience world, where traditional training methods are quite standardized. The testing process is also very uniform. People have been developing and testing this very precise set of behaviors for decades. So a change can show up clearly.

Conventional training procedures usually require a year or even two to develop a Novice competitor, another year or two for

---

1 From *Karen Pryor on Behavior: Essays and Research* (Sunshine Books, 1995)

Open competition, and another year or two for Utility, the highest testing level. Now people are clicker-training dogs to do the same behaviors in far less time. One person went from buying a dog to finishing all three levels of competition in a little over a year. Another dog owner taught her Australian cattle dog all the Utility hand signals for down, come, sit, and so on, in three minutes, by the clock. Another woman passed the three qualifying legs of the Novice competition, with very nice scores, with a ten-year-old Irish setter she'd trained for only three weeks. (Excuse me, but the breed is not known for intellect.) The dog died of old age shortly thereafter, and the owner said she wished she had found this wonderful method of communication earlier in his life. This is accelerated learning for trainer and trainee both.

Some people dismiss these reports of superfast learning as testimonials, but for me they have become diagnostic tools. When experienced traditional trainers "cross over" to clicker training—and tell me excitedly that something that used to take months just happened in a week, or a morning, or a minute—I can be pretty sure, even without seeing them work, that they've learned the two basic elements of clicker training. First, they have the clicker timing down pat, and second, they have also grasped the idea of raising criteria in small steps but quickly. Incidentally, another indicator that the new clicker trainer is using the technology correctly is that he or she spontaneously transfers the training from one species to another: "I taught my horse three things in a morning, and then I came into the house and clicker-trained the dog, the cat, and the guinea pig." Click!

Wouldn't it be fun to have data on the quickness with which clicker training works? I'm hoping some graduate student will make use of the competitive obedience community's rich database to scientifically compare conventional methods and the new technology.

Getting Rid of the Clicker

A frequent and understandable objection to the idea of clicker training is that you wouldn't want to be stuck having to click and treat for the rest of your subject's natural life. This, of course, is a misconception. The click is not intrinsic to maintaining the behavior; any old cue and any kind of reinforcer can do that. The click is for the *training* only. Once the learner has learned what you set out to teach it, you can put the clicker away. But you might use it again if you need to "explain" some new thing; you can communicate quite specific information with your clicker.

For example, my friend Patricia Brewington owns a clicker-trained Percheron gelding named James. Pat and her husband Daucy trained James with the clicker from babyhood through all his mature tasks of carrying riders, pulling wagons and sleighs, and hauling logs out of the woods. When James was fully educated, the clicker and food treats were no longer needed. James knew and complied with many voice cues and hand signals He visibly enjoyed praise and patting as reinforcers for work well done; and also ice cubes, playing with balls, ringing his sleigh-bells with his nose, coming into the barn, going out of the barn, being allowed to watch whatever the people were doing, and many other daily-life reinforcers.

One day James developed an abscess in his foot. The vet decreed that the foot should be soaked periodically. So Pat got a bucket of warm water, set it next to James, and put his foot into the bucket. James took it out. Pat put it in. James took it out. Now James is a very large horse, and Pat is a small woman. Physical force was not an option; and Pat almost never scolds her horses. What to do? She went in the house and found a clicker. She came back out to the barn. She put James's foot in the bucket—and clicked. Pat described his response metaphorically, as reinforcement trainers often do: "Ohhh! You mean *keep* my foot in the bucket. Oh, okay." No carrot was needed to seal the bargain; James just hadn't understood what was wanted, and when he did understand, he didn't mind doing it.

Clicker Training and Creativity

During my dolphin-training days I published a paper called "The Creative Porpoise: Training for Novel Behavior," describing some work we had done at Sea Life Park. This journal article became a psychology-classroom classic, used by professors year after year to pique students' interest in operant conditioning. Once again it wasn't entirely clear to me whether the capacity for inventing new behavior was special to dolphins or due to the training system. Now I can say with some certainty that creativity, or at least experimentation and initiative, is an intrinsic by-product of clicker training—in the trainer for sure, and in the learner as well.

The learner trained with a conditioned reinforcer is engaged in a kind of game: how to come up with behavior that will make the teacher click. If you watched a child playing this game, you wouldn't hesitate to say that it makes her want to learn—or even that it makes her think. Might that not also be true of animals?

I once videotaped a beautiful Arabian mare who was being clicker-trained to prick her ears on command, so as to look alert in the show ring. She clearly knew that a click meant a handful of grain She clearly knew her actions made her trainer click. And she knew it had something to do with her ears. But what? Holding her head erect, she rotated her ears individually: one forward, one back; then the reverse; then she flopped both ears to the sides like a rabbit, something I didn't know a horse could do on purpose Finally, both ears went forward at once. Click! Aha! She had it straight from then on. It was charming, but it was also sad: We don't usually ask horses to think or to be inventive, and they seem to like to do it.

Some owners of clicker-wise dogs have become so accustomed to canine initiative and experimentation that they rely on the dog "offering behaviors," both learned and new, as a standard part of the training process. Many clicker trainers play a game with their dogs that I have nicknamed "101 Things to Do with a Box" (or a chair, or a ball, or a toy). Using essentially the same procedure we used at Sea Life Park to develop "creativity" in a dolphin, in each session the dog is clicked for some new way of manipulating the object. For example, you might put a cardboard box on the floor and click the dog for sniffing it and then for bumping it with his nose, until he's pushing it around the room. The next time, you might let the dog discover that pushing the box no longer gets clicked but that pawing it or stepping over the side and eventually getting into the box is what works. The dog might also come up with dragging the box, or lifting and carrying the box. One dog, faced anew with the challenge of the box game, got all his toys and put them into the box. Click! My Border terrier once tipped the box over onto herself and then scooted around under it, creating the spectacle of a mysterious traveling box. Everyone in the room laughed hysterically, which seemed to please her. Some dogs are just as clever at coming up with new ideas as any dolphin could be; and dogs, like dolphins—and horses—seem to love this challenging clicker game.

Freedom from Fear

A much-debated element in clicker training, both by insiders and outsiders, is the absence of punishment. Conventional wisdom—and some psychologists—still hold that you should praise the good and punish the bad, and the result will be some kind of perfection in the middle. In fact, many of the problems people have in conventional training arise directly from the use of punishment. That Arabian mare had become unshowable because of a conventional method used for making a horse prick its ears: You swish a whip around its head (and hit it with the whip, now and then, back in the barn, so it knows the whip is dangerous). This mare had taken to laying her ears back and looking ugly instead of alert, a behavior that intensified with more punishment. Thus the remedial clicker training.

During training sessions, clicker trainers are finding if they mix reinforcement of desirable behavior with punishment or correction of behavior that they don't want, good things stop happening.

First, the accelerated learning stops, as the subject goes back to learning at the "normal" rate: slowly. Second, if they're not careful, the subject stops learning altogether—and stops *wanting* to learn, which is worse. As a child might drag himself unwillingly to school, dawdling along the way, dogs can show reluctance to perform, and stress when in the training situation. They pant, they yawn; they'd rather be elsewhere. But it's not unusual for clicker-trained dogs to actually initiate training sessions and to show enthusiasm by rushing eagerly into the training area.

I am not saying that clicker trainers never say no. Of course, you might reprimand a dog for eyeing the hors d'oeuvres on the coffee table, or restrain it with a leash on a crowded sidewalk. But we avoid using punishment, or its euphemism "correction," as a learning tool. During a training session the animal is free to take a chance, to make a guess, to try to come up on its own with reinforceable behavior. If it guesses wrong, fine. The worst that can happen is no click. In this safe arena learners quickly discover ways to show you the very best they are capable of, and that leads to wonderful results.

Learning and Fun

Here's another side effect of clicker training that people report over and over again: the global behavior of the learner changes. A punished or correction-trained animal learns to give the minimum necessary in order to stay out of trouble. These learners are "good soldiers": They do what they're told, and they never volunteer. Under this regimen, even if obedient, learners remain far more interested in their own doings and private life than in whatever you or any voice of authority might want. They are therefore not only vulnerable to distractions, they are *hoping* for distractions. Furthermore, when pushed too hard or punished too much, these learners get mad or quit. This is just the suite of behaviors we see in most household dogs, in many employees—and in kids in school.

In contrast, clicker training is fun, for trainer and learner both. Play is an important component. I've seen a profoundly low-functioning teenager laugh when she first got a click for a new behavior, and sign "play" when she saw the clicker, a sign her teacher didn't know she knew. Clicker trainers have learned to recognize play behavior in animals as a sign that the learner has become consciously aware of what behavior was being reinforced. When "the light bulb goes on," as clicker trainers put it, dogs gambol and bark, horses prance and toss their heads, and elephants, I am told, run around in circles chirping. They are happy. They are excited. That's reinforcing in itself. This event is predictable and replicable, and it is almost certainly accompanied by physiological changes, another fertile area for research.

When an animal participates at this level, the click acquires enormous value. It is *worth* much more than the food. Both the sound and the object that produces it become reinforcing. Here's an example. Debbie Davis is a clicker-training instructor who teaches disabled people to train their own service dogs. She herself is wheelchair-bound, and her service dog is a papillon, a little black and white toy breed about the size of a cat. The dog is very useful, in spite of his size. He can retrieve pencils, find the TV remote, and pull laundry out of the dryer. When he and Debbie go to training class, this little dog gets down off her lap, goes around under the chairs, gets into people's training equipment bags, and steals clickers: "Here, Mom—can't have too many of these, can we!"

Clicker Training for People

The laws of learning, like the laws of physics, apply to all of us, but visualizing the applications is not always easy. New clicker trainers often ask, with an embarrassed giggle, "Does this work with children?" (Or spouses?) Of course it could. But you have to learn how to do it. For example, shutting up about what you don't like, in order to wait for and reinforce behavior you do like, is counterintuitive and takes some practice.

Experiencing clicker training with a pet turned out to be a great place to start. People began to generalize their understanding. Seminar participants were making comments like these:

"I stopped jerking my dogs around—and then I realized what I was still doing to my kids!"

"I used to run my dental office staff with instruction and correction. Now I use shaping and reinforcement. You know what? The turnover dropped to zero."

"This has been nice for my dogs—but for *me* it has changed the way I deal with every single person in my life."

Clicker training, so simple and straightforward, had given people not just intellectual insight but also a new set of tactics to apply across many behavioral settings.

Nowadays this transfer of applications has become commonplace in the clicker community. Clicker trainers in the teaching professions—high school and college teachers, special ed teachers, physical therapists, caregivers in group homes—use the technology in their work. Parents of children with various developmental or physical deficits share with me what they are doing with and for their children, with their new skills. A mother is teaching her high-functioning autistic daughter to make appropriate social conversation, through shaping and reinforcement. Parents are improving the skills of their children with disabilities, from eating to dressing to walking and talking, with reinforcers and a marker signal.

Understanding reinforcement training can't repair physical or neurological deficits, and it won't replace the help that only skilled professionals can give, but it can make life easier for everyone. Parents are learning to shape appropriate behavior instead of accidentally reinforcing inappropriate behavior: to reinforce silence, not noise; play, not tantrums. It is not that they are "treating their children like animals," an ever-popular prejudiced attack; clicker training is not about animals or people. It's about better ways of teaching and learning.

Best of all, you don't need a Ph.D. to be an effective shaper. Recently I was driving home from an outing with my daughter and her family when her fourteen-month-old baby began to yell. He wasn't crying—yet, anyway—he was just making a very loud noise to protest the length of the drive and his incarceration in his car seat; and we were still twenty minutes from home. My seven-year-old grandson Wylie, in the backseat with his little brother, calmly got rid of the yelling by reinforcing longer and longer periods of silence. The marker? Wylie's grin. The reinforcer? One lick of Wylie's lollipop.

When I recently taught a course in shaping and reinforcement to about fifty educators, I asked them to do a shaping project. Sharon Ames, a speech and language pathologist, chose her three-and-a-half-year-old twins. Her shaping challenge was this: Though eight P.M. was the twins' supposed bedtime, it was taking three hours or more to get the little darlings to sleep every night.

Sharon introduced pennies, dropped into jars, as the reinforcer. In the morning each twin would be able to cash in the pennies for prizes. The first night the kids got a click—and a penny—for each stage of the go-to-bed process. Click for getting in the bath. Click for getting out, click for getting into pajamas, and so on. Then, when the lights went out, they got a click (and a penny, of course) if they were on their beds—not in them, just on them—every time Sharon came back in the room.

The first night she came in once a minute for the first half hour—that's thirty clicks—and then once every five minutes for another hour, by which time the children were asleep. The second night, she thinned the reinforcement schedule to every ten minutes, and within an hour, they were asleep. The third night the twins went to sleep right away. In three days the time it took to get the twins to bed and to sleep went from three hours a night to about twenty minutes, a comfortable level, and there it stayed. The twins endorsed the clicker. "Can we play the clicker game some more?" The reinforcer for Sharon and her husband was, of course, a real jackpot: a full night's sleep.

The Ames family then incorporated clicker training into their daily life. (Sharon told me they found it more effective to click very occasionally, but with bigger reinforcers.) Sharon's mother sometimes baby-sits for them, and Sharon showed her mother how to use the clicker with the twins. Then Sharon's mother adopted a dog. She complained about some behavior problems with her new pet. "Why don't you use the clicker?" Sharon said.

Her mother looked dubious. "Well, of course, it's *wonderful* for children, but do you really think it would work with dogs?"

Some More Human Applications

As I write this, I'm personally involved in developing two new human applications. One is the use of the clicker—in this case, an electronic "black box" clicker that plugs into a headset—in flight training. A click is not only more accurate, it permits reinforcement of behavior that is difficult to get at in other ways. For example, when turning to look at the instruments, you should take your hands off the airplane's controls to prevent accidentally turning the plane. However, as car drivers we've all learned to *never* take our hands off the wheel. Untraining a learned behavior is always much more tiresome than training a new one. A verbal reminder or correction takes far too long and comes too late. A click, however, can mark the smallest lift of the hands and pin it down forever.

A flight instructor can also click a student for initiative and for good thinking: for example, for glancing over the instrument panel *before* being reminded to do so. So the clicker can reward nonverbal behavior nonverbally, in the instant it's occurring. My son Michael Pryor, a pilot and the project developer, reports from preliminary data that in learning a skill such as instrument flying, clicking seems to build competency faster, and what's learned is retained well. Every pilot I've talked to since this project started pricks up his or her ears at the possibility of maintaining instrument rating and skills without having to go back into the simulator quite so often.

Clicker training is also much more enjoyable for the student. Michael Pryor says, "When you don't get clicked, and you thought you would, you escalate your movements. You try harder to find the thing you should be doing. And then when you do get a click, there's this neat feeling of *winning*. It's a lot better than getting yelled at."

My second project involves my consulting work with the New England Center for Children, in Southborough, Massachusetts. The New England Center, with a five-hundred-person staff and two hundred students, is one of the leading U.S. centers devoted to children with developmental deficits, especially autism. We are exploring the use of an event marker—sometimes a clicker, sometimes not—with children diagnosed with autism and other developmental deficits. The young and energetic teachers at the center, who supply around-the-clock, one-on-one, hands-on care for these challenging children, are college graduates, usually with a major in education or a related field. From the center they receive intensive on-the-job training in behavior analysis and its applications. What the clicker adds to their skills, at least to start, is a clear-cut piece of positive information for those children who can't or don't respond to spoken language; and feedback for the teachers on their own timing and escalation of criteria.

My year and a half of consulting has given me great hope that we will be able to document some of our preliminary observations. We've noticed that some behaviors that children with deficits are customarily taught seemed to benefit from using a marker signal along with a preferred edible treat. Such behaviors might include improved physical skills, improved eye contact, willingness to attend, and compliance with instructions. Some teachers I worked with used clicker training to reduce or eliminate resistance, in very easily upset children, to such necessary procedures as tooth brushing, haircuts, and taking temperatures. And sometimes the children really seem to be having fun.

I wish to emphasize that *none* of this is proven yet to scientifically acceptable standards. One great benefit of having the New England Center, a strongly research-oriented institution, take an interest in this exploration is that it might lift us clicker trainers out of anecdotal and descriptive uses of the application and make a data-based contribution to learning theory and its applications.

•   •   •

What's next? Trainers have been joining the Association for Behavior Analysis (ABA) and presenting papers and symposia at the annual meetings. The training community is meanwhile dipping further and further into the science, some even going back to school for advanced degrees. We are learning to name and recognize concepts we used only intuitively in the past, such as fluency, latency, and adduction.

I have been fascinated, through the ABA, to discover a group of researchers and educators who are seeing in their schoolrooms many of the phenomena we clicker trainers see. The applications they have developed are called Precision Teaching and Direct Instruction. The technology is tremendously effective. I visited one of the primary sites, a laboratory school in Seattle named Morningside Academy, established by Kent Johnson, Ph.D., and run by principal Joanne Robbins. The school takes only sixty children at a time. Most students at this school have been diagnosed with attention deficit disorder, hyperactivity, or learning disabilities. No child is accepted unless he or she is *at least* two years behind grade level in school. Morningside charges a respectable tuition, but it offers a full refund if the child does not improve by two full grade levels per year.

They have never had to give anyone their money back.

What do they do to make this happen? Everything a child needs to know to succeed academically is broken down into small steps. The steps are trained one by one, in very short sessions, with the kids tracking their own progress. The gains are self-reinforcing—you keep beating your own previous time and raising your own skill level—but they also can pay off in reinforcers such as computer time or computer games (which of course are all based on escalating reinforcement schedules).

Sometimes small gaps in a child's education cause endless problems, even though they are easily fixed. In one classroom I leaned over the shoulder of a nine-year-old boy who was working on writing the numbers from zero to nine as fast as he could, over and over, for one minute, for, in effect, a click. He's smart, but somehow the school system failed to teach him to write numbers clearly and quickly. That little glitch in his training might have made a nightmare out of everything in his future career, from algebra to jotting down a girl's phone number. So fix it now.

That of course is just a tiny sample of this educational application of operant conditioning. The Morningside Model is spreading. Dr. Johnson and his partner, T.V. Joe Layng, Ph.D., are also running a much larger program in the Chicago school system, and there are other related programs elsewhere.

The transformation of school systems so that they actually work will be, I hope and expect, partly due to science, and innovators like Layng and Johnson, and partly due to parents. To make *any* of this work, you have to do something yourself. You cannot just hire an expert and say "Fix my dog," or "Fix my child," or even, "Fix the school system." You are the primary trainer. This is a participation sport.

Clicker Training Around the World

I believe the general public's attitude about this branch of science has changed considerably in the last fifteen years. There are still people who shudder at the very name of Skinner, which conjures in their minds some amalgam of *Brave New World,* mind control, and electric shock. But for every one of those there are many more people who are comfortable with the concept of positive reinforcement.

Some just give it lip service, of course. As Kathleen Weaver, the founder of the Internet Clicker List, points out, we trainers mean much more by the term *clicker training* than mere *clicker-using.* Clicker "users," who may call themselves "positive" or "motivational" trainers, might borrow that particular device, the clicker, to mark their choice of specific behaviors. But then they go on using punishment, physical coercion, and all the other aversive tools of conventional training as well.

Clicker *trainers,* by contrast, may use any sort of stimulus as a marker signal; they attach no superstitious magic to the clicker itself. But they also consciously avoid superstitious behavior (such as escalation of punishment). And their toolkit consists of the full panoply of shaping, positive reinforcement, and related operant conditioning laws. They are the ones, whether working with children or adults, or horses or dogs, or any other animal, who reap the benefits—rapid learning, long retention, happy, participating learners, and pure fun—of the technology we call clicker training.

Perhaps the multitudinous minds working on the new technology will come up with a more distinguished and generic name for this approach than clicker training; I hope so. But that ultimate identifier might not be in English. Thanks to the Internet, clicker training has become a planetary phenomenon. The Clicker List might hear one day from sled-dog trainers in Finland who use reindeer bone whistles (metal ones freeze to your lips) to click their dogs, and the next day from a poodle owner in Bosnia or a veterinarian in Singapore. Or an Englishwoman writes of teaching her pet hedgehog to fetch. In 1998 my website, www.dontshoot-thedog.com, was receiving 150,000 "hits" a month, from at least forty different nations monthly.

There is a buzz, a feeling of excitement, in all this shared communication, experimentation, and discovery. The early days of development of any technology must have been much the same: the early days of flying, or of radio, when kids in remote farms tuned in on crystal sets if only to hear a distant time signal. We are pioneering. We don't know where we will end up yet.

Aaron Lynch, author of *Thought Contagion*, quotes from communication engineering science on the special communication involved in the spread of a technology. For a technology to spread fast, he says, it has to have three characteristics: It must be easy; it must have visible benefits to the user; and it must be something that can be learned in small increments. Clicker training fits the bill. That's certainly what happened for the dog owners. When people see a conventionally trained dog in action, they tend to say, "That must have taken years, I could never do that." Or, "My dog could never be that smart." In contrast, people see a clicker-trained dog in action and exclaim: "How did you do that? Can I do it? Show me. Let me try."

You can't tell, in advance, what particular event will be the hook for each new group of users. Alexandra Kurland's horses and clients, working in a big boarding stables with dozens of other people around every day, were learning all kinds of new skills and at tremendous rates; but it was all dismissed by the on-lookers as "that crazy clicker stuff"—until she taught a horse to retrieve. To fetch a toy, like a dog. Suddenly everyone in the stables had to have a retrieving horse. "How'd you do that? Can I do it too?"

In a recent e-mail Alex wrote, "It's done. We can't put the genie back in the bottle now. This is going to be fun."

I hope she's right about the genie and the bottle.

I *know* she's right about the fun. It has always been fun.

Resources

The Association for Behavior Analysis
1201 Oliver Street
Western Michigan University, 213 West Hall,
Kalamazoo, MI 49008
Tel. 616-387-8341
www.wmich.edu/aba
The scientific society for behavior analysts; publications, journals, and regional and international annual conferences.

The Association of Pet Dog Trainers
P.O. Box 385
Davis, CA 95017
Tel. 1 800-PET-DOGS
www.apdt.com
Positive training methods emphasized. Newsletter, annual conference.

Aubrey Daniels Associates
3531 Haversham at Northlake
Tucker, GA 30084
Tel. 1 800-223-6191
Applied behavior analysis in the corporate setting.

The Cambridge Center for Behavioral Studies
336 Baker Avenue
Concord, MA 01742
Tel. 978-369-2227
www.behavior.org
A bridge between behavioral science and the public. The powerful website can steer you toward the information you need and the people who have it in any area of applied behavioral science, from autism to animal husbandry to education to industrial safety.

Dog and Cat Book Catalog
Direct Book Service
701 B Poplar Street
P.O. Box 2778
Wenatchee, WA 98807-2778
Tel. 800-776-2665
www.dogandcatbooks.com
A very complete source for pet-training books and videos, including small-press and out-of-print titles.

The International Association of Marine Animal Trainers
1720 South Shores Road
San Diego, CA 92019
Membership is limited to active trainers, but the magazine, research journal, and annual conference are open to all.

Morningside Learning Systems
1633 Twelfth Avenue
Seattle, WA 98122
Tel. 206-329-9412
A source for information on Precision Teaching and related educational applications.

The New England Center for Children
33 Turnpike Road
Southboro, MA 01772

Tel. 508-481-1015
www.necc.org
Specializing in applied behavior analysis, serving children with autism, pervasive developmental deficit, and related disorders.

www.onlearn.com
David Feeney's online learning website. Fun and cutting edge. Manage your own behavior with online interactive charting and reinforcement. Smoking, weight loss, and the like.

Sunshine Books, Inc.
49 River Street
Waltham, MA 02453
Tel. 800-47CLICK or 781-398-0754
www.clickertraining.com
Publisher and distributor of books and videos on positive reinforcement, clicker training, Precision Teaching, and other human and animal behavioral applications. On-line ordering and free catalog by mail.

Acknowledgments

I'd like to thank Murray and Rita Sidman for their friendship and encouragement and for Murray's detailed editorial commentary on the first edition of *Don't Shoot the Dog!* and on the revisions. His wise and kindly guidance contributed vastly to this more informed and—I hope—more useful new edition. Any new or retained errors, however, are solely mine.

I'd like to thank Phil Hineline, for inviting me to speak at the ABA meetings in 1992 and thus opening up new paths; the late Ellie Reese, for forcing me to take myself and my work more seriously; Myrna Libby and Vincent Strully, for giving me the opportunity to work at the New England Center for Children; and the late Kenneth Norris, for making me a dolphin trainer and getting me into all this trouble in the first place.

I'd also like to thank Jon Lindbergh and Gary and Michele Wilkes for the series of seminars we put on together, across the United States and Canada, in the early 1990s. It was a huge effort, yet enormous fun as well, and I learned a lot about the fascinating problem of training trainers.

Since then the community of clicker trainers has continued to develop and expand this application of behavioral science in a blend of brilliance, creativity, and warmheartedness. I'm especially grateful to Kathleen Weaver, for maintaining the longest-running flame-free Internet list I know of, the Clicker List; and to Kathleen Chin, for organizing and sponsoring so many valuable seminars and conferences. I'm also grateful to all the clicker-training innovators, especially Corally Burmaster (competition dogs and horses), Steve White (police dogs), Carolyn Clark and her staff (pet owners), Morgan Spector (obedience), Alexandra Kurland (horses), Diana Hilliard (service and show dogs), Melinda Miller (horses), Lana Mitchell (herding dogs), Steve Layman (falconry), Jim and Amy Logan (llamas), Myrna Libby (children), Mike Pryor (adults), and Bob and Marian Bailey (all ages and all species). The next round of expansion is just beginning; it's a joy to have so many friends and colleagues sharing the trip.

About the Author

KAREN PRYOR is a writer and a behavioral biologist. She was a founder and pioneering dolphin trainer at Hawaii's Sea Life Park, where she befriended and worked with B. F. Skinner and Konrad Lorenz. She enjoys an international reputation as a scientist in both behavioral psychology and marine mammal biology. She has served as a federal commissioner on the Marine Mammal Commission and has consulted on human and animal behavior and learning for organizations ranging from NASA to the National Zoological Park. She is a trustee of the Cambridge Center for Behavioral Sciences.

Her first book, *Nursing Your Baby,* has sold more than two million copies; her daughter Gale Pryor has updated a revised edition. Pryor is also the author or coauthor of some thirty scientific papers. She is the founder and CEO of Sunshine Books, Inc., a behavioral publishing company.

Pryor has three children, six grandchildren, and a Border terrier. She lives in the Boston area.

Index

Further reading:

O'Neill, Amanda
Doggy Problems Solved
9781842862179, Interpet Publishing, 2009

Nester, Mary Ann
Smart Tricks
9781842862186, Interpet Publishing, 2009

Arrowsmith, Claire
The Sit, Down, Come, Heel, Stay and Stand Book
9781842861912, Interpet Publishing, 2008

Evans, Jim
What If My Dog...?
9781842861165, Interpet Publishing, 2006

Tennant, Colin
Mini Encyclopedia of Dog Training & Behaviour
9781842861141, Interpet Publishing, 2008

Pryor, Karen
Clicker Training for Dogs
9781860542824, Ringpress Books, 2002